A Retreat With
Gerard Manley Hopkins and Hildegard of Bingen

# Other titles in the
# A Retreat With... *Series:*

# A RETREAT WITH
# GERARD MANLEY HOPKINS AND
# HILDEGARD OF BINGEN

## *Turning Pain Into Power*

## Gloria Hutchinson

**St. Anthony Messenger Press**
Cincinnati, Ohio

Estés, and Ballantine Books, a division of Random House, Inc.

Excerpt from *The Creators* by Daniel Boorstin, copyright ©1992 by Daniel Boorstin, used by permission of Random House, Inc.

Excerpts from St. Hildegard of Bingen: *Symphonia: A Critical Edition of the Symphonia armonie celestium revelationum.* Edited and translated by Barbara Newman. Copyright ©1989 by Cornell University. Used by permission of the publisher, Cornell University Press.

Excerpt from "Here I Am, Lord" by Daniel L. Schutte, copyright ©1981 by Daniel L. Schutte and New Dawn Music, P.O. Box 13248, Portland, OR 97213, used by permission of Oregon Catholic Press.

Excerpts from *Soul Friend: The Practice of Christian Spirituality* by Kenneth Leech (San Francisco: Harper & Row, 1980), used by permission of HarperCollins Publishers.

Excerpts from *Migraine: Understanding a Common Disorder*, by Oliver Sacks, M.D., copyright ©1985 by Oliver Sacks, reprinted in the United States by permission of the University of California Press, and in Canada, the United Kingdom and Australia by permission of International Creative Management.

Excerpt from *The Spiritual Lives of Great Composers*, by Patrick Kavanaugh, copyright ©1992 by Patrick Kavanaugh, used by permission of Sparrow Press.

Excerpts from *Sermons and Devotional Writings of Gerard Manley Hopkins*, edited by Christopher Devlin, S.J. (London: Oxford University Press, 1959), reprinted by permission of Oxford University Press.

Cover illustrations by Steve Erspamer, S.M.
Cover and book design by Mary Alfieri

ISBN 0-86716-251-1

Copyright ©1995, Gloria Hutchinson

All rights reserved.

Published by St. Anthony Messenger Press
Printed in the U.S.A.

# Contents

# *Introducing* A Retreat With...

Twenty years ago I made a weekend retreat at a Franciscan house on the coast of New Hampshire. The retreat director's opening talk was as lively as a long-range weather forecast. He told us how completely God loves each one of us—without benefit of lively anecdotes or fresh insights.

As the friar rambled on, my inner critic kept up a sotto voce commentary: "I've heard all this before." "Wish he'd say something new that I could chew on." "That poor man really doesn't have much to say." Ever hungry for manna yet untasted, I devalued any experience of hearing the same old thing.

After a good night's sleep, I awoke feeling as peaceful as a traveler who has at last arrived safely home. I walked across the room toward the closet. On the way I passed the sink with its small framed mirror on the wall above. Something caught my eye like an unexpected presence. I turned, saw the reflection in the mirror and said aloud, "No wonder he loves me!"

This involuntary affirmation stunned me. What or whom had I seen in the mirror? When I looked again, it was "just me," an ordinary person with a lower-than-average reservoir of self-esteem. But I knew that in the initial vision I had seen God-in-me breaking through like a sudden sunrise.

At that moment I knew what it meant to be made in the divine image. I understood right down to my size eleven feet what it meant to be loved exactly as I was. Only later did I connect this revelation with one granted to the Trappist monk-writer Thomas Merton. As he reports in *Conjectures of a Guilty Bystander*, while standing all unsuspecting on a street corner one day, he was overwhelmed by the "joy of being...a member of a race in which God Himself became incarnate.... There is no way of telling people that they are all walking around shining like the sun."

As an absentminded homemaker may leave a wedding ring on the kitchen windowsill, so I have often mislaid this precious conviction. But I have never forgotten that particular retreat. It persuaded me that the Spirit rushes in where it will. Not even a boring director or a judgmental retreatant can withstand the "violent wind" that "fills the entire house" where we dwell in expectation (see Acts 2:2).

So why deny ourselves any opportunity to come aside awhile and rest on holy ground? Why not withdraw from the daily web that keeps us muddled and wound? Wordsworth's complaint is ours as well: "The world is too much with us." There is no flu shot to protect us from infection by the skepticism of the media, the greed of commerce, the alienating influence of technology. We need retreats as the deer needs the running stream.

### An Invitation

This book and its companions in the *A Retreat With...* series from St. Anthony Messenger Press are designed to meet that need. They are an invitation to choose as director some of the most powerful, appealing and wise mentors our faith tradition has to offer.

Our directors come from many countries, historical

eras and schools of spirituality. At times they are teamed to sing in close harmony (for example, Francis de Sales, Jane de Chantal and Aelred of Rievaulx on spiritual friendship). Others are paired to kindle an illuminating fire from the friction of their differing views (such as Augustine of Hippo and Mary Magdalene on human sexuality). All have been chosen because, in their humanness and their holiness, they can help us grow in self-knowledge, discernment of God's will and maturity in the Spirit.

Inviting us into relationship with these saints and holy ones are inspired authors from today's world, women and men whose creative gifts open our windows to the Spirit's flow. As a motto for the authors of our series, we have borrowed the advice of Dom Frederick Dunne to the young Thomas Merton. Upon joining the Trappist monks, Merton wanted to sacrifice his writing activities lest they interfere with his contemplative vocation. Dom Frederick wisely advised, "Keep on writing books that make people love the spiritual life."

That is our motto. Our purpose is to foster (or strengthen) friendships between readers and retreat directors—friendships that feed the soul with wisdom, past and present. Like the scribe "trained for the kingdom of heaven," each author brings forth from his or her storeroom "what is new and what is old" (Matthew 13:52).

## The Format

The pattern for each *A Retreat With...* remains the same; readers of one will be in familiar territory when they move on to the next. Each book is organized as a seven-session retreat that readers may adapt to their own schedules or to the needs of a group.

Day One begins with an anecdotal introduction called "Getting to Know Our Directors." Readers are given a telling glimpse of the guides with whom they will be sharing the retreat experience. A second section, "Placing Our Directors in Context," will enable retreatants to see the guides in their own historical, geographical, cultural and spiritual settings.

Having made the human link between seeker and guide, the authors go on to "Introducing Our Retreat Theme." This section clarifies how the guide(s) are especially suited to explore the theme and how the retreatant's spirituality can be nourished by it.

After an original "Opening Prayer" to breathe life into the day's reflection, the author, speaking with and through the mentor(s), will begin to spin out the theme. While focusing on the guide(s)' own words and experience, the author may also draw on Scripture, tradition, literature, art, music, psychology or contemporary events to illuminate the path.

Each day's session is followed by reflection questions designed to challenge, affirm and guide the reader in integrating the theme into daily life. A "Closing Prayer" brings the session full circle and provides a spark of inspiration for the reader to harbor until the next session.

Days Two through Six begin with "Coming Together in the Spirit" and follow a format similar to Day One. Day Seven weaves the entire retreat together, encourages a continuation of the mentoring relationship and concludes with "Deepening Your Acquaintance," an envoi to live the theme by God's grace, the director(s)' guidance and the retreatant's discernment. A closing section of Resources serves as a larder from which readers may draw enriching books, videos, cassettes and films.

We hope readers will experience at least one of those

memorable "No wonder God loves me!" moments. And we hope that they will have "talked back" to the mentors, as good friends are wont to do.

A case in point: There was once a famous preacher who always drew a capacity crowd to the cathedral. Whenever he spoke, an eccentric old woman sat in the front pew directly beneath the pulpit. She took every opportunity to mumble complaints and contradictions—just loud enough for the preacher to catch the drift that he was not as wonderful as he was reputed to be. Others seated down front glowered at the woman and tried to shush her. But she went right on needling the preacher to her heart's content.

When the old woman died, the congregation was astounded at the depth and sincerity of the preacher's grief. Asked why he was so bereft, he responded, "Now who will help me to grow?"

All of our mentors in *A Retreat With...* are worthy guides. Yet none would seek retreatants who simply said, "Where you lead, I will follow. You're the expert." In truth, our directors provide only half the retreat's content. Readers themselves will generate the other half.

As general editor for the retreat series, I pray that readers will, by their questions, comments, doubts and decision-making, fertilize the seeds our mentors have planted.

And may the Spirit of God rush in to give the growth.

*Gloria Hutchinson*
*Series Editor*
*Conversion of Saint Paul, 1995*

# Getting to Know Our Directors

## *Introducing Gerard Manley Hopkins*

The seminarian's practice sermon was not going well. His voice teetered like a nervous tightrope walker. If only he could be swallowed up by the pulpit's maw! His fellow Jesuits were contorted by suppressed laughter. They seemed to misconstrue his eccentric eloquence deliberately. Gerard Manley Hopkins, pale as Marley's ghost, could not escape the consequences of his singularity.

He had tried to guide his listeners through a meditation on the multiplication of the loaves and fishes. But his habit of mixing earthy with exalted examples (as disparate as salmon and seraphs) short-circuited their piety. He later wrote of his sermon:

> People laughed at it prodigiously. I saw some of them roll on their chairs with laughter. This made me lose the thread, so that I did not deliver the last two paragraphs right but mixed things up. The last paragraph, in which "Make the men sit down" is often repeated, far from having a good effect, made them roll more than ever.[1]

Through his life, as priest and poet, Hopkins would gamely fulfill the vocation of being misunderstood. He might easily have altered his voice to blend in with the choir. Instead, he went on singing like a rara avis in a flock of common song sparrows.

Born at Stratford, Essex, in England, on July 28, 1844, Hopkins was the first of nine children. He soon evidenced the literary and artistic qualities of his parents. At Balliol College, Oxford, the young Anglican was drawn to the flame of the Oxford Movement. (Although it began as a doctrinal and theological self-examination by certain Anglicans, the movement led Dr. John Henry Newman and others into the Roman Church.) Against his family's will, Hopkins was received into the Catholic Church by Newman in 1866.

Upon joining the Jesuits two years later, Hopkins burned his poetry and resolved to write no more. His goal was to become a perfect priest by giving himself totally to God. His pen might have remained idle had his heart not been stirred by a newspaper account of a shipwreck in December 1875. The *Deutschland*, a passenger ship from Germany en route to England, had broken apart on the rocks during a snowstorm off the English coast.

One of the sixty-four passengers who lost their lives was a German Franciscan nun who had cried out at the peak of the storm, "O Christ, Christ, come quickly!" Her prayer impelled Hopkins to meditate on the paradoxes of suffering and death. After seven fallow years, the young Jesuit gave birth to a long narrative poem startling in its originality and unwavering faith.

"The Wreck of the Deutschland" took Gerard Manley Hopkins six months to write. The editor of the in-house Jesuit magazine, to which Hopkins submitted the poem, took much less time to reject it. This initial repudiation of his talent proved prophetic. Although Hopkins continued to produce poems until his death at forty-four, his work was never published in his lifetime. When his friend Robert Bridges brought out a Hopkins collection thirty years after the Jesuit's death, it took ten years to sell out all seven hundred fifty copies.

How much pain repeated literary rejection cost Hopkins we can only guess. He insisted that a writer could be happy even though denied his just renown. Yet "when this happens it is an evil in itself and a thing which ought not to be and that I deplore, for the good work's sake rather more than the author's."[2]

He was a poet ahead of his time, an eccentric as out of place among the late Victorians as a feminist theologian at the Council of Trent. Not until after World War I did any number of readers begin to catch on to Hopkins' brilliance and spiritual depth. Today his poetry continues to dazzle or perplex high school and college students of yet another generation.

But we who have come to meet Gerard Manley Hopkins as our retreat director are intrigued by the person as well as his work. We are drawn to him as a fellow pilgrim on the rough road to Jerusalem. We want a closer look at the complex Catholic hidden behind that finely-drawn ascetic face. We seek consolation and guidance from this holy priest who clung to Christ even in the depths of depression.

> And my lament
> Is cries countless, cries like dead letters sent
> to dearest him that lives alas! away.[3]

Who exactly was Gerard Manley Hopkins and why should we listen to him? He was a convert who, like Thomas Merton seventy years later, fell in love with Catholicism and became an ardent believer. (Before becoming a Trappist, Merton reflected on Hopkins as the subject of his proposed doctoral studies.)

Hopkins was an amateur naturalist whose

appreciation for the "thisness" of specific plants, trees, birds, waterways, landscapes and seasons was scientific and artistic. Like contemporary creation theologians, he would decry as sinful the despoilation of the earth.

> O if we but knew what we do
> When we delve and hew—
> Hack and rack the growing green![4]

He was a teacher of rhetoric, Greek and Latin, who pined after popularity with his students. To that end, he once laid down in the classroom and instructed a student to drag him across the floor by his heels to "illustrate the death of Hector" in Homer's *Iliad*. His odd practical jokes may have made him more of a curiosity than a mentor to his students. Hopkins was so scrupulous about grading essays and exams that he often wound up with a wet towel wrapped around his aching head. Such mundane tasks drained and deflated him during his final years in Ireland.

Catholic to the core, Hopkins was a devoted admirer of Mary and the saints, a lover of the Eucharist and the sacred heart of Jesus, a true Jesuit whose every effort was dedicated *A.M.D.G.* (*Ad majorem Dei Gloriam*, "To the greater glory of God"). He advised giving alms "to the point of sensible inconvenience" and pointed out that humanitarians are sometimes better at practicing the works of mercy than are the Christians who preach those works.

Hopkins was an artist and a musician, an avid walker and canoeist, a reliable correspondent and an admirer of physical beauty in women and men. As biographer Bernard Bergonzi says of him, the evidence suggests that Hopkins was homosexual in inclination and perfectly celibate in life: that he was aware of sexual excitement at physical beauty but equally aware of its religious sublimation, and he wondered why he had to be a eunuch for the kingdom of heaven's sake.[5]

He was a man of slight build and haunting face. His character is best described as "the handsome heart" (the title he gave one of his poems). Hopkins would in some ways identify with those women who today read Clarissa Pinkola Estes' *Women Who Run With the Wolves*, hoping to reclaim their "wildish nature." Like these women, the Jesuit poet spent much of his adult life doing work that seemed to him worthless, work that dried him out. There was never enough time for the theology and prosody books he wanted to write, for the fullness of friendships and communion with nature he so desired.

As a perfectionist whose inner critic was rarely off duty, Hopkins needed large doses of affirmation from others. Yet many of his fellow Jesuits thought him odd or even slightly daft. The poet's primary support came from intimate friends like Robert Bridges, Canon Richard Watson Dixon and the elderly Miss Cassidy, to whose genteel home he sometimes retreated.

Most importantly, Hopkins was a profound appreciator of life who suffered frequent melancholia and depression. When we read his letters and dark sonnets written in Dublin, our hearts shrink from so much pain so well endured. He speaks of his "fagged mind and a continual anxiety," "a great trial of broken sleeps," "a wretched state of weakness and weariness," "fits of sadness...[that] resemble madness."

Without benefit of worldly success, the consolations of family life or the elation of fully investing his gifts, Gerard Manley Hopkins remained hopeful, often cheerful and ever faithful. When he died of typhoid fever (probably caused by faulty plumbing in the Jesuit residence hall), Hopkins' final words were: "I am so happy. I am so happy."

## *Introducing Hildegard of Bingen*

The community has gathered for evening recreation. Their hands busied with needlework or artistry, the veiled women warm the room with their chatter. Sitting slightly apart from them, the abbess is as content as a mother hen with a healthy brood. Amused by an anecdote about a befuddled monk, she laughs long and commends the storyteller. A young novice arches her eyebrow, signaling her disapproval.

Mother Hildegard is not one to let a teaching opportunity escape her. Secure in her knowledge of human anatomy and psychology, she takes the novice aside to enlighten her.

> Laughter is a healthy thing. It promotes respiration and breath is life; it carries blood through tissues and muscles, liver and spleen. It is true that raucousness makes the spleen fat. But laughter is from the heart.[6]

Before the novice has time to respond, Hildegard takes the younger woman's head in her hand and says, "There is a tightness in your neck, daughter. You must have more fresh air and more wine in which to dip your bread. God wants us to have joy in our souls and health in our bodies." The novice smiles despite herself. Mother Hildegard is a hard woman to resist.

She was born in 1098 at Bermersheim (Germany), the youngest of ten children. When she was eight, her parents turned her over to Jutta von Spanheim, an anchoress attached to the Benedictine monastery at Disibodenberg.

Here Hildegard learned to read Latin and pray the psalms.

After taking religious vows, the young Hildegard was tutored by a monk of St. Disibod named Volmar. Jutta's holiness had meanwhile attracted many noblewomen to join her. The hermitage became a monastery. In 1136, upon Jutta's death, the community elected Hildegard as abbess. Like a willow by a running stream she flourished in that office for the next forty-three years.

Five years later Hildegard's unique vocation began to shine. She had been gifted with visions since childhood. Yet she had not recounted them, fearing that she would become a laughingstock. Only Jutta was privy to the divine revelations made to Hildegard. Later Volmar and the aristocratic nun Richardis von Stade were taken into the abbess' confidence. They convinced her to heed the command given her in a vision. "Write what you see and hear! Tell people how to enter the kingdom of salvation!"

Cheered on by her two friends, Hildegard transcribed her visions on wax tablets. Volmar corrected and copied the text into book form. This first of three visionary books would be entitled *Scivias* (*Know the Ways*). In it Hildegard named the source of her astounding wisdom. She said it came from the *umbra viventis lucis*, the reflection of the living Light. The Light bypassed her external senses, communicating directly with her soul. She never fell into a rapture or otherwise lost her normal consciousness during these visions. As she describes it:

> And as the sun, the moon, and the stars appear in water, so writings, sermons, virtues, and certain human actions take form for me and gleam within it.[7]

The wisdom recorded in *Know the Ways, The Book of Life's*

*Merits* (1158-1163) and *The Book of Divine Works* (1163-1173) guided readers through the mysteries of the Bible, the complexities of the moral life and the narrow gate into the kingdom. The living Light entrusted this knowledge to "a poor little female" (as she styled herself) because the male leaders of Church and state were too "lukewarm and sluggish in observing the justice of God." On Hildegard's strong shoulders fell the mantle of prophet, teacher, preacher and diplomat.

And that was just the beginning. As her creativity began to flow like the Jordan, she produced poetry and liturgical music, medical and herbal guides, an encyclopedia of science and three decades worth of sermonic correspondence to popes and emperors, priests and religious, laity of every hue. In her spare time, she invented an Unknown Language (complete with 900 newborn words and a Germanic glossary).

Could a wonder woman of Hildegard's brilliance fail to evoke opposition in twelfth-century European society? Certainly not. Among those who tried to rein her in were the abbot of St. Disibod's, superior of the men's monastery to which Hildegard's community was subordinated. When Abbot Kuno refused to allow the abbess to found a new community at Rupertsberg, she undermined him with two strategies. One was to go over his head to ecclesiastical authorities with whom her noble family had connections. The other was to take to her bed with a mysterious ailment that paralyzed her. She informed Kuno that her illness would not abate until he stopped preventing her from fulfilling God's will. The abbot was no match for Wonder Woman!

We retreatants are well aware of Hildegard's renewed reputation as a churchwoman to be reckoned with and a mystic whose works still speak with power. We are drawn to her as a spiritual mother. We may not know her face and form. Yet her soul sings to us of how to live in harmony with our Creator, with creation and within ourselves.

Like Gerard Manley Hopkins, Hildegard draws us by the startling expression of a faith that has been tempered in the fires of "humdrum suffering." The abbess endured chronic pain associated with her visions. In a letter to the young monk Guibert of Gembloux, she writes:

> But because of the constant sickness that I suffer, I sometimes get tired of writing the words and visions that are there revealed to me. Yet when my soul tastes and sees them, I am so transformed that, as I say, I forget all pain and trouble.[8]

Oliver Sacks, neurologist and author of *Awakenings*, says Hildegard's writings and illustrations reflect the "many varieties of visual aura" that inaugurate certain attacks of migraine headaches. He praises her allegorical interpretations of her visions—while interpreting them physiologically himself. Sacks views Hildegard as having a "privileged consciousness" that can turn what others experience as "banal, hateful, or meaningless" (i.e., a migraine attack) into the substance of a "supreme ecstatic inspiration."[9]

Before undertaking each of four preaching journeys (1155-1171), the abbess suffered debilitating illnesses. She felt that death was near. However, she was assured in a vision that her time had not yet come. Encouraged by a chorus of angels and saints, Hildegard got up from her sickbed. At age fifty-nine she set out on horseback to preach God's justice to those monks who were oppressing her own community. This "manly task" of confrontation required every ounce of strength she could muster.

Sickness, depression, opposition and misunderstanding were Hildegard's familiars throughout her life. The deaths of her two most beloved friends (Volmar and Richardis) burdened her with a terrible grief. Her love for the Church was constantly tested by her knowledge of the laxity, sexual immorality and power politics indulged in by so many clerics and religious. In the final year of her life, Hildegard was subjected to a trial worthy of Job himself. Her community was placed under interdict by Abbot Kuno, depriving the nuns of Eucharist, the Divine Office and the last rites. (Hildegard refused to exhume the body of a nobleman buried on the monastery grounds. Abbot Kuno insisted that the man had been excommunicated. Abbess Hildegard insisted that the man had repented and received absolution before his death.)

Although the abbess managed to get the interdict lifted after six months of debilitating appeals, she died six months later. Hildegard became one with the living Light. Her armor of trusting hope had served her well. She wrote:

> [Melancholy] does not know a trusting hope in God, but instead is seized by an evil compulsion to greater and greater distress.... And yet, it is restrained by bliss. And people are thus taught that they should not continue in a situation of melancholy.[10]

## Placing Our Directors in Context

The worlds of Hildegard of Bingen and Gerard Manley Hopkins were as different from each other as they are from our own. Yet what our directors have in common—between them and with us—retains its value in whatever time or place. While Hildegard was appreciated more widely in her day than was Hopkins in his, both have come into their own among later generations. The voice, words and witness of each mentor speak with power to those who love God and have (or pray to have) trusting hope in God.

## Hildegard of Bingen's World

The Middle Ages span the period between the fall of the last emperor of the Western Roman Empire (A.D. 76) to the Turkish conquest of Constantinople (1453), capital of the Ottoman Empire. Hildegard's eighty-one years (1098-1179) were lived in the later Middle Ages during the time of the first two Crusades to liberate the Holy Land. The Church had already been divided by the Great Schism (1054) between East and West. Feudalism, the economic, political and social system based on land ownership, divided people into the distinct classes of serfs, vassals and overlords.

As a Benedictine, Hildegard followed the *Rule* of St. Benedict, father of Western monasticism. During her formative years, she would have absorbed Benedict's image of God as a just Judge, his belief that the will of God is made known through the abbot (or abbess), his love of liturgical prayer and *lectio divina* (or "receiving the revelation of God" through reading, meditating and responding to God's word). She, like all Benedictines, would have summed up her monastic life as *ora, labora, vita communis* or prayer, work, common life.

In the year Hildegard was born, a major reform of monasticism began with the founding of the Abbey of Citeaux. These Benedictines called themselves

Cistercians (Trappists). They refused to accept land grants from the wealthy, insisting instead on turning swamps into "golden meadows" by their own labor. Both Saint Bernard of Clairvaux and Pope Eugenius III, contemporaries of Hildegard, were Cistercians. When Hildegard sought confirmation for her visions, she wrote to Bernard. If he, the leading churchman of the twelfth century, validated her gift, she would be secure.

Bernard not only gave his blessing to the in-progress manuscript of *Scivias*, he also praised Hildegard's visions before Church leaders gathered at the synod at Trier (1147-48) and persuaded Pope Eugenius to give the abbess his apostolic blessing. That letter, like an Academy Award to an obscure actress, made Hildegard a celebrity. New postulants converged on St. Disibod's, which soon outgrew its capacity. This unexpected growth, together with a vision of the hill known as Rupertsberg near Bingen, convinced Hildegard to found her own independent monastery there.

Although the abbess often complained that she lived in an "effeminate age," she was not implying that women dominated either Church or state. Quite the opposite was true. Women were considered the weaker, less competent sex; they owed obedience to husbands and/or male religious and secular authorities. Paul's dictum—"I permit no woman to teach or to have authority over a man; she is to keep silent" (1 Timothy 2:12)—left little room for women of Hildegard's brilliance to shine. Only if she could "prove" that her visions came directly from God would a woman be heeded by the Church.

While Hildegard lived during a renaissance in learning, a time when the arts and sciences were flourishing, she and other women were denied access to a university education. Her only formal learning was provided by Jutta and Volmar. Yet she wrote such scientific handbooks as the *Book of Simple Medicine* (or *Physica*) and the *Book of Compound Medicine* (or *Causes and Cures*). Where did she gain the prerequisite knowledge? Downplaying her own intellect, Hildegard insisted that everything she wrote came from God. She was merely the "poor little female" who took dictation from the living Light.

As a member of the aristocracy, Hildegard found it easier to speak the truth to secular than to hierarchical power. She advised King Conrad III of Germany to "be a good servant to God," and chastised his nephew Frederick Barbarossa as "an infant, and a madman" for backing his own papal candidate against Pope Alexander III. She dared to oppose the emperor even though Frederick had extended his imperial protection to the Rupertsberg monastery. When the emperor persisted in his schismatic stance, Hildegard threatened him with all the prophetic thunder of Jonah in Nineveh. "Woe, woe to the malice of wicked men who defy me! Hear this, king, if you wish to live; otherwise my sword shall smite you,"[11] she wrote. It is a measure of Barbarossa's respect for Hildegard that although he did not heed her advice, neither did he withdraw his imperial protection from her and her sisters. (Frederick later died during the Third Crusade when he, Philip Augustus and Richard the Lionhearted massed their forces against the Sultan of Egypt and Syria.)

As a member of an agrarian society, Hildegard was keenly interested in the growing of herbs and grains, the cycles of nature, the "juiciness" of living things and the interdependence of human beings with all of creation. "In the midst of all other creatures/humanity is the most significant/and yet the most dependent upon/the others," she observes.[12] She felt an intense kinship with the lush greenness of earth and coined the term *viriditas* for the greening power of Christ, who revives all that is withered.

Hildegard was a precursor of the thirteenth and fourteenth century Rhineland mystics of Germany and the Low Countries: Mechtild of Magdeburg, Gertrude of Helfta, Henry Suso and Meister Eckhart. These mystics embraced a unifying cosmological and prophetic spirituality that often integrated religion and science, art and human justice. All sought union with God as the center of their being; they were fascinated by the intimate intercourse between humanity and divinity. As Eckhart observed, "Cherish in yourself the birth of God, and with it all goodness and comfort, all rapture, reality, and truth will be yours."[13]

Like Hildegard herself, the Rhinelanders favored right-brain imagery that was feminine and often erotic.

In our retreat, we look to Hildegard as a seer, one familiar with the stunning gold-clad woman she envisioned as Sapientia. Aptly enough, the Latin *sapientia* comes from *sapere*, meaning to savor or taste. And Hildegard, by temperament and profession, was a relisher of wisdom. She harvested abundant images from Proverbs, Ecclesiastes, the Song of Songs. Her grounding in wisdom literature, which was common in the Middle Ages, enabled her to live in harmony with the perfect order of God's creation. The originality of the variations she played on the ancient tradition is unmatched in any age.

A retreat with Hildegard of Bingen is an opportunity to be refreshed and restored by the "bubbling fountain."

> The soul that is full of wisdom
> is saturated with the spray of
> a bubbling fountain—God himself.[14]

## Gerard Manley Hopkins' World

The Victorian Age, or late nineteenth century, designates the sixty-four-year reign of Queen Victoria (1837-1901). It was a time of economic, social and cultural transformation in which agrarian England became an industrialized state. Smoke-belching factories and intrusive railways scarred a once-pastoral scene. Workers swarmed to the cities, seeking wealth yet finding squalor. Social critics like Thomas Carlyle and Charles Dickens argued against the prevailing mindset of profits over people. Change blustered through the land, upsetting the applecarts of tradition.

With the publication of Charles Darwin's *On the Origin of Species* (1859), many Victorians confronted a crisis of faith. If the scriptural accounts of the creation were not literally true, was humanity actually made in the divine image after all? Did the scientific theory of evolution contradict religious faith? The poets of the age wrestled with their doubts and often took refuge in introspection or a contemplative sadness. "In Memoriam," Alfred, Lord Tennyson's reflections on the sudden death of a friend, echoes his struggles to believe despite "The faithless coldness of the times."

The poems of Gerard Manley Hopkins (1844-1889) appear as shafts of light against the gloomy backdrop of his contemporaries' melancholy and doubt. Even when he is most anguished, Hopkins doubts not God but himself. He is almost painfully aware of God's active presence in creation. Nature is a powerful witness testifying to "God's Grandeur"; to be indifferent to the testimony is to deny God the praise that is due. However, even when people are consumed by trade and toil, each new morning offers a fresh opportunity to be present at the creation.

Oh, morning, at the brown brink eastward,
    springs—
Because the Holy Ghost over the bent
    World broods with warm breast and with ah!
    bright wings.[15]

Hopkins' England was the heart of a great empire,
stretching out to extensive possessions in Australia, New
Zealand and North America, India and Africa. The British
Empire engendered pride in Hopkins, whose soul was
always stirred by his country's seafaring adventures. His
father, Manley Hopkins, also a poet, was a marine
insurance adjuster who instilled Gerard with patriotism
and a love of all things nautical. (The family's wealth,
ironically enough, depended upon the ill fortune of those
who suffered disasters at sea.)

Though Hopkins' family was privileged and well
educated, he did not divorce himself from the working
classes. While serving among the urban poor of Liverpool
and Glasgow, he was sickened by the multiple injustices
heaped on them. "It made even life a burden to me to
have daily thrust upon me the things I saw," he wrote to
a friend.[16] He urged Robert Bridges (who was not a
Christian) to give alms—in the form of money or that
kind of service for which he was best suited. With wry
humor, Hopkins observed that the corporal works of
mercy received universal approval although not
universal application. "Even Walt Whitman nurses the
sick," he quipped in a letter to Bridges on January 29,
1879. (Whitman, then making a name for himself in
America as the poet of democracy and individualism,
envisioned a new religion of comradeship that he would
lead. He was the poet most admired by Hopkins.)

As a Jesuit, Gerard Manley Hopkins was formed in the
spirituality of Saint Ignatius Loyola, a sixteenth-century

Spaniard who surrendered his sword to our Lady at her shrine at Montserrat and took up a life of prayer, penance, solitude and service. Out of his retreat cave at Manresa came Ignatius' *Spiritual Exercises*, a manual of prayer and interior renewal. Based on a dialogue between the retreatant and a director, the *Exercises* guide meditations on the life of Christ, examinations of conscience, vocal and mental prayers designed to free the soul for discernment of God's will. Ignatius believes it is possible for each of us to know and "perfectly fulfill" the will of God. (We will see how this conviction spurred Hopkins, the highstrung thoroughbred.)

Ignatian spirituality is also characterized by a sacramental awareness of creation. One biographer of the saint, Pedro de Ribadeneira, observed that Ignatius, at the sight of a single leaf or common earthworm, could "reach through into things which lie beyond the senses." The founder urged young Jesuits to seek God in the enjoyment of landscapes, pleasant walks, good conversations and other pursuits that exercise the senses. In this regard especially, Gerard Manley Hopkins was perfectly obedient to his spiritual father's teaching.

In his own small way, Hopkins fulfilled the Jesuit's apostolic mission of teaching and serving as missionaries. He spent five hard years in Ireland educating the sons of the middle class at University College, Dublin. His aesthetic sensibility, intellectualism and physical slightness made him a misfit among these largely rough-and-ready young men. His patriotism too was sorely tried as he discerned that the Irish patriots contending with England for home rule had a just cause. The conflict filled him with "world-sorrow."

A second conflict of the day cost Hopkins dearly. The Oxford Movement or Tractarian Movement cut a deep rift through the Church of England, to which the Hopkins family had always belonged. It began in 1833 with an investigation by certain Oxford intellectuals into the nature of the Anglican Church. Members of the movement feared the Church's subordination to the state. They defended the Church's independence and lobbied for a return to the High Church traditions of the seventeenth century. John Henry Newman's *Tracts for the Times* (1833) and W. G. Ward's *The Ideal of a Christian Church* (1844) moved many Anglicans toward the Roman Catholic Church. In 1845 Newman caused an uproar by resigning as the Anglican vicar of St. Mary's and converting to the Roman Church.

Strongly influenced by Newman and his 1864 autobiographical work defending his conversion (*Apologia pro Vita Sua*), the young Hopkins agonized over his own possible conversion. He was "in love with" the doctrine of the real presence of Christ in the Blessed Sacrament, and felt that God had already decided for him that he belonged in the Catholic Church. His parents were horrified—both at his conversion and his subsequent decision to join the Jesuits. They battered him with rational arguments and emotional appeals. Gerard stood firm. In a letter to his mother, he revealed that every new letter from either parent "breaks me down afresh.... You might believe that I suffer too."[17]

Hopkins' singularity, so achingly clear in his poetry, makes him a poor fit in any established literary or spiritual category. Yet he continues to influence and inspire writers as diverse as Jesuit peace activist Daniel Berrigan and English critic Anthony Burgess. Quotes from Hopkins crop up like jack-in-the pulpits on the literary and religious landscapes year after year. Once heard, his voice is rarely forgotten.

In our retreat, we look to Hopkins as a saint who saw and praised the beauty of Christ shining through creation. We listen to him as a poet who spoke the language of the soul with intensity. We befriend him as a man of sorrows who communicated an unfailing appreciation for the gift of life.

A retreat with Gerard Manley Hopkins is an opportunity to be kindled with grace in order to burn brightly and live justly. For the kindled Christian:

> Acts in God's eye what in God's eye he is—
> Christ—for Christ plays in ten thousand places,
> Lovely in limbs, and lovely in eyes not his
> To the Father through the features of men's faces.[18]

## Notes

[1] *Sermons and Devotional Writings of Gerard Manley Hopkins*, ed. Christopher Devlin, S.J. (London: Oxford University Press, 1959).

[2] *Gerard Manley Hopkins: Selected Letters*, ed. Catherine Phillips (Oxford: Oxford University Press, 1991), p. 100.

[3] Untitled, *Poems of Gerard Manley Hopkins*, ed. W.H. Gardner (New York: Oxford University Press, 1948), p. 109.

[4] "Binsey Poplars," ibid., p. 83.

[5] See Helen Vendler, "Cliffs of Fall Frightful," *New York Times Book Review*, May 1, 1977, p. 14.

[6] Ingeborg Ulrich, *Hildegard of Bingen: Mystic, Healer, Companion of the Angels*, trans. Linda M. Maloney (Collegeville, Minn.: The Liturgical Press, 1993), p. 44.

[7] Barbara Newman, *Sister of Wisdom: St. Hildegard's Theology of the Feminine* (Berkeley, Calif.: University of California Press, 1987), p. 7.

[8] Ibid.

[9] Oliver Sacks, M.D., *Migraine: Understanding a Common Disorder* (Berkeley, Calif.: University of California Press, 1985), p. 108.

[10] Ulrich, p. 231.

[11] Newman, p. 13.

[12] Gabriele Uhlein, *Meditations With Hildegard of Bingen* (Sante Fe, N.M.: Bear & Co., 1983), p. 87.

[13] *Meister Eckhart*, trans. Raymond Bernard Blakney (New York: Harper & Row, 1941), p. 103.

[14] Uhlein, p. 63.

[15] "God's Grandeur," *Poems*, p. 70.

[16] *Letters.*

[17] Ibid., pp. 53-54.

[18] Untitled, *Poems*, p. 95.

# DAY ONE
## *Catching the Windhover*

### *Introducing Our Retreat Theme*

Ordinary life is a prudent shoplifter. While we are attending to other things, it depletes our inventory. If we fail to nab the culprit in time, we become the victims of a first-class felony. The crime? We have been robbed of our commitment to follow Christ with all our hearts, minds and souls. The means by which the criminal deed was done? Tools of the trade include: chronic worry, overwork, depression, exhaustion, sickness, failures and losses of every hue.

Oddly enough, these same tools, in the hands of the saints, achieve the opposite effect. They do not deplete; they build up inner treasure. They do not weaken; they generate strength. They prove Paul's assertion: "For whenever I am weak, then am I strong" (2 Corinthians 12:10b).

Whenever we detect the shoplifter's shadowed movements, it is time to consult the experts. They know what we are up against. They have the gift of tongues (prayer, poetry, music) to communicate wisdom. As friends of God, Gerard and Hildegard want nothing more than to help us appreciate the healing channels of creation, creativity and communion. By these means, they will train us in the art of "turning pain into power."

Gerard Manley Hopkins loved "The Windhover" best of all his poems. The title refers to a small hawk that hovers in the wind. In the windhover, Hopkins saw both Christ and himself. Today as our poet-mentor opens the retreat we pray that we too may be "stirred for a bird."

## Opening Prayer

> Priest-brother,  poet-friend,
> Ignatian mentor, help us mend
>
> Hearts divided, pummeled, pale
> Hearts anxious, failing, frail
>
> Train our eyes to catch the Hawk!
> Instruct our feet to Falcon-stalk!
>
> Let your life kindly lead
> Out of darkness in our need
>
> Christ! Ride on astride the air
> Thrust us through gray banks of care.
>
> Amen, Jesus.
> Amen, Gerard.
>
> Let the retreat begin.

# RETREAT SESSION ONE

We are gathered in a sunroom, enveloped in glass and light. The retreat house is in a valley; we can lift up our eyes to the source of our help. Through an open window we overhear a brook humming to itself. The spring air seduces us with the scent of fresh-cut cedar. Bird songs skitter along the surface of the day, baiting our curiosity. The morning is free from care.

Having had our coffee and made ourselves comfortable, we are eager to meet the first of our two retreat directors. The pairing of mentors is engaging. (While it would be good to watch Jane Torville or Christopher Dean skate solo, it is far better to see them as a team.) Mother Hildegard, with her characteristic esteem for holy priests, has invited Father Hopkins to precede her.

He enters with a brisk step and an edgy smile. Poet-thin, in clerical black, he has the intensity of one for whom there is never enough time. He drops the leather-bound notebook in which his poetry is recorded. As a retreatant rushes to pick it up, Hopkins quips, "If I could get a fish to bite that quickly, we'd all be dining on salmon for lunch."

The laughter we give him makes him feel more at ease. His voice, slight like his body, loosens up. He stands at a lectern, needing the security of a prop. Despite his Roman collar and clerical distance, we sense his affection. Hopkins is glad to be here with us. We are, after all, not the captive audience of the pew or the classroom.

Hopkins opens his book, devoutly draws the Sign of the Cross on its pages and speaks to us in poetry. Like a pop singer who accedes to his fans' wish to hear their all-time favorite, the Jesuit gives us "God's Grandeur."

> The world is charged with the grandeur of God.
>     It will flame out, like shining from shook foil;
>     It gathers to a greatness, like the ooze of oil
> Crushed. Why do men then now not reck his rod?
> Generations have trod, have trod, have trod;
>     And all is seared with trade: bleared, smeared

with toil;
And wears man's smudge and shares man's smell:
the soil
Is bare now, nor can foot feel, being shod.

In this sonnet, the first eight lines or octet describe how
God's presence is shown forth in creation. Humanity,
however, is often oblivious to the divine presence; people
fail to see their misery as a result of sin or a way of
atoning for it.

Greed and selfishness have left their mark on nature.
In the concluding six lines or sestet of the poem, Hopkins
draws his own conclusion about the dreariness of the
industrial age and the new life which is ever available to
us.

And for all this, nature is never spent;
There lives the dearest freshness deep down
things;
And though the last lights off the black West went
Oh, morning, at the brown brink eastward,
springs—
Because the Holy Ghost over the bent
World broods with warm breast and with ah!
bright wings.[1]

The sound of "God's Grandeur" is as intoxicating as
dandelion wine. Hopkins' sprung rhythm, akin to early
Anglo-Saxon poetry, gives the lines an earthy, elemental
appeal. The poet nearly sings his composition, rocking
slightly on his heels. Sensing our fogginess to his
message, Hopkins leans on the lectern and converses
informally.

"God's Grandeur" had come to him while he was
teaching at St. Beuno's in North Wales in 1877. Teaching
was burdensome—perhaps because he tried so hard. He

longed to write more poetry and music; there was never enough time or energy for the things he wanted to do "on his own account." His digestive system was troublesome; life at times seemed "dank as ditch-water." But every day he returned to the daily round of duties and devotions his vocation required of him. He knew that "Until you prefer God to the world and yourself you have not made the first step."[2]

When his time was his to squander or invest, Hopkins would wander the hillsides in the valley of Clwyd. He once described his method of responding to nature in these words:

> ...for a certain time I am astonished at the beauty of a tree, shape, effect etc., then when the passion...has subsided, it is consigned to my treasury of explored beauty, and acknowledged with admiration and interest ever after, while something new takes its place in my enthusiasm.[3]

While responding to the beauty of the landscape, Hopkins had suddenly seen the connection with the Ignatian *Exercises*. In his "Contemplation for Obtaining Love," Ignatius urges retreatants to recognize that "all things are charged with God." If we touch them with awareness, they will throw off sparks, exude moisture and ring out like church bells. Tuning in to the grandeur that can shatter humanity's misery and overcome its greed, the poet felt the "dearest freshness deep down things." He was refreshed at the "warm breast" of the maternal Holy Spirit.

We nod with understanding. Our mentor decides to take us deeper into his experience of God in creation. Turning to another page written at St. Beuno's, he proclaims selected lines from "The Windhover," dedicated "To Christ our Lord." This time his face flushes as he proclaims his love for his "chevalier."

> I caught this morning morning's minion, king-
>   dom of daylight's dauphin, dapple-dawn-drawn
>     Falcon, in his riding
>   Of the rolling level underneath him steady air,
>     and striding...
>     ...My heart in hiding
>   Stirred for a bird,—the achieve of, the mastery of the
>     thing![4]

In the sestet that follows these lines, Hopkins describes how he willingly submits to Christ the King, whose "brute beauty" sheds spiritual fire on those who have eyes to see him in the figure of the windhover. The poet compares his own soul to seemingly dead embers that "Fall, gall, gash gold-vermilion." Hopkins' own inner fire is then revealed.

Again our mentor pauses, smiling in an uncondescending way at the confusion mirrored in our faces. He apologizes for the singular way in which he expresses his spirituality. Each poet is, of course, a unique species. To find Christ in that poet's lines we must stalk him with purpose, patience and attention.

In catching with his eyes the windhover astride the morning air, Hopkins had grasped the particular "make of it." The bird's unfettered, ecstatic activity had revealed its "suchness." The kestrel's beauty is beyond expression. Yet the poet-priest's heart is so stirred he must attempt to communicate his devotion. He has been lifted above his workaday anxieties; he has known the thrill of swinging through the morning sky with the powerful, masterful, majestic windhover. It is an epiphany to be shared, praise to be sung.

Laughing with excitement at the memory of his encounter, our director closes his book, saying, "Any questions?" Before any of us can formulate an acceptable response, Hopkins adds, "If so, the Holy Spirit will answer them. Go outside into the air. Wade in the brook. Study the sky. Smell the earth. Lie in the grass. Look sharply. The Hawk awaits you."

Gerard Manley Hopkins, his dark eyes shining like awakened embers, gives us a mindful blessing and leaves us to our own resources. The air still crackles after he is gone. Without speaking, we go out to make vital connections.


## For Reflection

- *In what ways has creation refreshed and restored you in times of exhaustion, disappointment or depression? Take time now to be outside in a peaceful place. Rest. Breathe from deep within the center of your body. Re-create in every refreshing detail (what did you see? feel? smell? hear? touch?) one particular experience of being restored by creation. Stay with the experience for as long as you like. Breathe in peace. Breathe out gratitude to our Creator-God.*

- *For you, how is the world "charged with the grandeur of God"? How have you helped others to experience the grandeur?*

- *How might the image of the Holy Ghost "brooding" over the world affect your prayer? your ability to trust? your ministry?*

- *In what ways will you be guided by Hopkins' habit of opening himself to landscapes, waterways, plants, birds, skies and adding to his "treasury of explored beauty"?*

- *What feelings, attitudes and actions does "The Windhover" call forth in you? What image of Christ in creation is most loving for you? How will you communicate that image to others?*


## Closing Prayer

(To be experienced in whatever cathedral of creation or rustic chapel your present circumstances make possible.)

Choose one or more of these paired words of wisdom—from the word of God and the work of Gerard Manley Hopkins. Read, reread, pray and make the words your own. Invite the Holy Ghost to brood over you with "warm breast" and "bright wings."

**From the word of God:**
> Then I looked, and there was a white cloud, and seated on the cloud was one like the Son of Man, with a golden crown on his head, and a sharp sickle in his hand! (Revelation 14:14)

**From the work of Hopkins:**
> I walk, I lift up, I lift up heart, eyes,
> Down all that glory in the heavens to glean our Saviour;[5]

**From the word of God:**
> God made the wild animals of the earth of every kind, and the cattle of every kind, and everything that creeps upon the ground of every kind. And God saw that it was good. (Genesis 1:25)

**From the work of Hopkins:**

Glory be to God for dappled things—
For skies of couple-colour as a brindled cow....[6]

**From the word of God:**

When they had heard the king, they set out; and there, ahead of them, went the star that they had seen at its rising, until it stopped over the place where the child was. When they saw that the star had stopped, they were overwhelmed with joy. (Matthew 2:9-10)

**From the work of Hopkins:**

Look at the stars! look, look up at the skies!
O look at all the fire-folk sitting in the air![7]

*Notes*

[1] "God's Grandeur," *Poems*, p. 70.

[2] *Letters*, p. 66.

[3] Ibid., p. 18.

[4] "The Windhover," *Poems*, p. 73.

[5] "Hurrahing in Harvest," ibid., p. 74.

[6] "Pied Beauty," ibid., p. 74.

[7] "The Starlit Night," ibid., p. 70.

# Day Two
## Becoming a Feather

### Coming Together in the Spirit

In her best-selling book *Women Who Run With the Wolves: Myths and Stories of the Wild Woman Archetype*, Clarissa Pinkola Estés draws deeply on her experience as a Jungian analyst and a *cantadora* (keeper of the old stories) in the Latina tradition. Her purpose is to help women reconnect with the "wild woman," that is, the integral instinctual nature, in their unconscious; or, as she also calls the process, doing the "work of soulful reclamation." When a woman has done this hard inner work, Estés says, she can readily tap into her inner power, passionate creativity and timeless knowing and fulfill her "moral obligation" to live the truth she sees.

According to Dr. Estés, the one who enables women to act out of their deepest insight may be called *La Que Sabe* (The One Who Knows). Once a woman has been breathed on by *La Que Sabe* (an archetypial figure), that woman is changed. She has reclaimed her soul from the cultural traps of sexism and overdomestication. As Dr. Estés puts it:

> Our work is to show we have been breathed
> upon—to show it, give it out, sing it out, to live in
> the topside world what we have received through
> our sudden knowings from story, from body, from

dreams and journeys of all sorts.[1]

Eight centuries ago there lived a woman whose extraordinary visions enabled her to speak and act with power in a male-dominated age. She called herself, in the idiom of her day, "a poor little female." From mid-life on, however, she left little doubt that she had been "breathed upon." Hildegard of Bingen not only ran with the twelfth-century wolves. She often led the pack.

## Defining Our Thematic Context

On Day One, Gerard Manley Hopkins invited us to immerse ourselves in creation—especially when we are worn out, worn down, feeling less than ourselves. By opening ourselves to "God's grandeur," we can at times disperse the inner clouds, replacing them with appreciation and gratitude. Our mentor suggested that we build up a "treasury of explored beauty" to strengthen our interconnectedness with nature. He urged us to get out in the air and to keep a sharp eye out to "catch the Windhover," who is Christ.

Today our mentor is Hildegard of Bingen. She will share her wisdom on becoming a feather on the breath of God. Through her humble trust in God, Hildegard shows us how to gain ascendancy over negative forces that bear down on us. She says that care for creation begins with our own bodies, which are temples of the Holy Spirit.

## Opening Prayer

Abbess-sister, poet-friend,
Benedictine mentor, help us tend

Inner gardens, psychic wells
Wildish nature within ourselves.

Herbal gardens, wholesome brooks
Green-lush landscapes, sea-green nooks.

Let your life lightly lead
Plant in us the Spirit's seed.

Breathe on us, All-Knowing-One!
Lift these feathers to the Son!

Amen, Holy Spirit.
Amen, Hildegard.

Let the retreat continue.

# Retreat Session Two

There is a stir in the sunroom as a tall nun of striking appearance strides in, carrying a basket over her arm. This cannot be Hildegard of Bingen. She is too young; her authority is too slender. It is perhaps Richardis von Stade, beloved friend and protegee of our mentor. She informs us that Hildegard would like each of us to receive a small gift made by members of the Rupertsberg community. (This is Abbess Hildegard's way of casting her net over us before she makes her entrance.)

Richardis graciously presents us with miniature scrolls of wheat-colored parchment, tied with green ribbons. As we open them, we are delighted with the calligraphy employed by the sisters in inscribing the introduction to Hildegard.

Listen: There was once a king sitting on his throne.
Around him stood great and wonderfully beautiful
columns ornamented with ivory, bearing the
banners of the king with great honour. Then it
pleased the king to raise a small feather from the
ground and he commanded it to fly. The feather
flew, not because of anything in itself but because
the air bore it along. Thus am I a feather on the
breath of God.[2]

The vision is unsigned. However, a pale gray dove's
feather has been affixed at the bottom with sealing wax.

While we have been comparing our scrolls, so
uniquely executed by hands at prayer, Hildegard has
entered and seated herself regally on a low stool. She is
garbed in one of those feast-day habits that offended her
more ascetic contemporaries in the cloister. Her veil is of
white silk crowned by a tiara. Her strong hands are
adorned with gold rings. She may have rubbed her
cheeks with a bit of beet juice for wholesomeness' sake. A
consecrated virgin, she believes, should not always hide
the splendor of her femininity.

Because today is a Marian feast, Mother Hildegard
begins with a sung "Antiphon for the Virgin" of her own
composition. She invites us to join her; most of us are too
fascinated by her contralto voice and the strangeness of
the music to do anything but listen.

Morning bursts into light,
the golden bough into green.
Let grief be put to flight—
exult, virgin queen!
Lend your hand with a shout
of high auroral praise,
and lift us frail ones out
of our old bad ways.[3]

(As a medieval moralist, she is simply reminding us that we all need help to remain on the narrow way.)

"Daughters and sons," she says, her voice warm as the sun. "Know from the start that the wisdom I share with you comes not from this poor creature you see before you but from the living Light. If I had communicated my visions out of a desire for personal gain, God would not allow me to be here with you today." With the confidence of the truly humble, she continues:

> God works where God wills, for the honor of the divine name and not for the honor of earth-bound mortals. But I am continuously filled with fear and trembling. For I do not recognize in myself security through any kind of personal ability. And yet I raise my hands aloft to God, that I might be held by God, just like a feather which has no weight from its own strength and lets itself be carried by the wind.[4]

To validate her own weakness, Hildegard reminds us that she was often sick, sometimes paralyzed, frequently depressed in her lifetime. With a smile that acts as a tonic on us, she adds, "And yet God has always made me alive again, even to this day."[5]

One of the primary ways in which God revived Hildegard "seventy times seven times" was by instilling in her soul an awareness of the interdependence of all living things. Like Francis of Assisi, who came after her, she knew that the cosmos and everything in it was related to her: the sun, the wind, the orchards and forests, flowers and stones, fields and valleys, rivers and hills, fire and rain, lambs, bears and all flying creatures. To live in right relationship with creation is graciously to accept the gift God holds out to us each new day. For Mother

Hildegard, God and creation are Lover and beloved. She compares their mutual love to a marriage which is abundantly fruitful.

In her sensitivity to physical beauty and health, Hildegard is closely aligned with Gerard Manley Hopkins. Both mentors resonate to the splendor of an unsullied landscape and of a well-configured human body. As Hopkins once observed, "I think then no one can admire beauty of the body more than I do,"[6] so Hildegard, in her *Book of Divine Works*, lavishly praises "The Articulation of the Body." For both mentors, physical beauty is a testimony to the presence of God in us and in the world.

Mother Hildegard stands now, revealing her ample stature. She speaks with authority; we attend her every word.

> O human, see then the human being rightly: the human being has heaven and earth and the whole creation in itself, and yet is a complete form, and in it everything is already present, though hidden.[7]

Our mentor believes profoundly in the holiness of the body, sees it as a reflection of the pattern inherent in the cosmos. In the roundness of the head and symmetry of the entire body, she sees the Divine Artist's hand. The soul, Hildegard believes, "takes possession of the whole body." When soul and body act in agreement, the soul soars into the heavens like the birds of the air. By nourishing ourselves with the contemplation of beauty and the wisdom of the Scriptures, we are "invisibly nourished and fortified, just as a fish that has been fortified by air and rushing water can live for a time in water without nourishment."[8]

Because the Creator honored humanity through the

Incarnation, in which God's Son appeared in our own human flesh, blood and bone, we are to honor, care for and protect our bodies. Mother Hildegard informs us that she could give us an entire month's retreat exploring the medical and biological wisdom revealed to her by the living Light. However, instead of offering us a six-course feast-day meal, she will entice us with a few appetizers. (Let those who crave wisdom look further into her writings: *The Book of Divine Works* and *Book of Compound Medicine*, or *Causes and Cures*.)

First we are to eat slowly and chew well, making sure our diets are fortified with whole grains and made more salubrious by the informed use of herbs and spices. We should eat enough good food to truly refresh ourselves so that there "be no lack of joy in our souls." On this point, Hildegard adds: When someone is suffering from a great sorrow, that person should eat heartily of those foods that agree with him or her, in order to be revived by food, since sorrow has weighed the person down so much.[9]

Our bodies should also be respected in their need for sufficient sleep. Mother Hildegard's "cure for insomnia" is nightly to read in a prayerful state of mind, with hand laid over the heart, the first words of John's Gospel: "In the beginning was the Word." Then we are to pray:

> Lord, almighty God, in the abundance of your goodness you have awakened me through the breath of life. By the most holy garment of our tender human nature with which your Son was clothed on my account, I entreat you: Do not let it happen that I am plagued any further through the bitterness of this unrest. But for the sake of the love of your only begotten Son, free me from this affliction through your merciful help, and defend me against all the snares of the spirits of the air![10]

When we feel ourselves growing hot with anger, we should contemplate the tame creatures of the earth such as the lamb or the cow. When we feel ourselves growing cold with sorrow, we should gaze at a green landscape and absorb the healing green through our eyes. When we feel ourselves being pulled down through depression, we must not give in to this "spiritual paralysis" that "fetters the soul's forces." Against depression we must marshal the forces of repentant tears, sincere prayer and good works. In this way, the body draws strength from the power of virtue just as the "clouds draw up the waters of the Earth and then rain them down again."[11] (Hildegard's advice will be of little use to those whose clinical depression is caused by a chemical imbalance in the brain. She and her contemporaries were unaware of the physiological causes of depression.)

If we drive ourselves too hard, refusing to rest when we are tired or eat when we are hungry or taking the air when we are feeling stifled, we are leaving ourselves open to the predator called melancholy.

> But those who are ill with melancholy are like hard earth that can only be turned with great difficulty by the plow; in their thoughts they are full of anger, sorrow and internal contradiction. For when they are unable to pull themselves together through the power of their own souls, they can have no joy in their own deeds.[12]

As a long-term strategy against inordinate sadness, our mentor advises us to become increasingly conscious of the duality within ourselves. When body and soul contend with one another, or when self-will opposes God's will, depression is often the result. In wisdom we must value harmony within and without, daily absorbing the greenness of tranquillity and peace.

As we care for our bodies, so we must care for the earth that so generously sustains us. Hildegard's expression is stern as she tells us, "The earth should not be injured. The earth should not be destroyed."[13] When we do not tend to our kin in creation, we endanger our own survival.

A signal from Richardis alerts our mentor to the time. "Enough," Mother Hildegard says. "If I burden you with too much wisdom at once, you will not float like feathers; you will drop like stones to the bottom of the pond. Go outside now. Be light and airy. Pray to Mary, our luminous mother:

> Ask for us life. Ask for us radiant joy. Ask for us the sweet, delicious ecstasy that is forever yours."[14]

With a dramatic sweep of her festal garments, Hildegard of Bingen leaves us dazzled.

## *For Reflection*

- *At this stage of your life, do you experience yourself more as a "feather on the breath of God" or a stone at the bottom of a pond? Why? If you are a stone, who or what might help you to "lighten up"?*

- *Because of her visions, Hildegard had the courage and trust to speak in the light what she learned in the dark. Her earthiness encouraged her to trust her intuition. What visions, dreams or journeys have enabled you to trust the light within yourself? How might you be able to help at least one other person to do likewise?*

- *What is your response to Hildegard's belief in the holiness of the human body? Her emphasis on attending to the body's needs—especially when we are low? Her intuition that the soul "takes possession of the whole body"? What practical applications will you make of Hildegard's wisdom—for yourself, for others?*

- *For you, how are good stewardship of the body and of the earth connected? What images of the interconnectedness of all living things suggest themselves to you? Choose one image to pray over with heart, head and hands. (You might draw, paint, mold, construct, write, choreograph or create a "living sculpture" with others.)*

- *Hildegard and Gerard Manley Hopkins behold Mary as the luminous mother of creation; she is intimately united with all living beings through her mothering of God's Son. Other poets compare her to the elements that sustain us: air, water, light, growing things. She is the green bough that scatters our grief. Describe your own present relationship with Mary. How might the insights of our retreat directors help that relationship to blossom or take deeper root?*

## Closing Prayer

(To be experienced in any place of natural beauty—preferably on a day when the breath of the wind can be enjoyed. If you choose, float a feather or fly a kite.)

Choose one or more of these paired words of wisdom—from the word of God and the work of Hildegard of Bingen. Read, reread, pray and make the words your own. Ask God to help you become "a feather on the breath of God."

**From the word of God:**

Then the Lord God formed man from the dust of the ground, and breathed into his nostrils the breath of life; and the man became a living being. (Genesis 2:7)

**From the work of Hildegard:**

Now this human is rightly called "alive,"
because as long as the person exists
on the breath of the Holy Spirit,
the person is indeed, life.[15]

**From the word of God:**

For it was you who formed my inward parts;
    you knit me together in my mother's womb.
I praise you, for I am fearfully and wonderfully
    made. (Psalm 139:13-14)

**From the work of Hildegard:**

For just as the word of God has penetrated everything in creation, the soul penetrates the whole body in order to have an effect on it. The soul is the green life-force of the flesh. For, indeed, the body grows and progresses through the soul, just as the Earth becomes fruitful through moisture.[16]

**From the word of God:**

Praise him, sun and moon;
    praise him, all you shining stars!
Praise him, you highest heavens,
    and you waters above the heavens!

Praise the LORD from the earth,
    you sea monsters and all deeps,
fire and hail, snow and frost
    stormy wind fulfilling his command!
(Psalm 148:3-4; 7-8)

**From the work of Hildegard:**
And I am the fiery life of the essence of God: I flame above the beauty of the fields; I shine in the waters; I burn in the sun, the moon, and the stars. And, with the airy wind, I quicken all things vitally by an unseen, all-sustaining life.[17]

## Notes

[1] Clarissa Pinkola Estés, Ph.D., *Women Who Run With the Wolves: Myths and Stories of the Wild Woman Archetype* (New York: Random House [Ballantine Books], 1992), p. 33.

[2] Hildegard of Bingen, *Manuscript Two* (Weisbaden: Hessische Lantesbiblioter). See also Hildegard of Bingen's *Book of Divine Works*, ed. Matthew Fox (Sante Fe, N.M.: Bear & Co., 1987), p. 347.

[3] Hildegard of Bingen: *Symphonia: A Critical Edition of the Symphonia armonie celestium revelationum*, ed. and trans. Barbara Newman (Ithaca, N.Y.: Cornell University Press, 1989), p. 121.

[4] *Book of Divine Works*, p. 348.

[5] Ibid., p. 349.

[6] Phillips, p. 131.

[7] Ulrich, p. 85.

[8] *Book of Divine Works*, p. 111.

[9] Ulrich, p. 135.

[10] *Book of Divine Works*, p. 334.

[11] Ibid., p. 108.

[12] Ulrich, p. 163.

[13] Uhlein, p. 78.

[14] Ibid., p. 117.

[15] Ibid., p. 113.

[16] *Book of Divine Works*, pp. 96-97.

[17] *Sister of Wisdom*, pp. 69-70.

# DAY THREE
## *Relishing the Juice and Joy*

### *Coming Together in the Spirit*

In his later years, Michelangelo Buonarroti regretted that he had given his life to "painting and sculpture, labour and good faith." He wished that he had taken up the making of matches as a child rather than the drawings for which his father punished him. However, even as he complained in a sonnet: "Melancholy is my joy/And discomfort is my rest," Michelangelo betrayed a relish for the artist's vocation.[1] Had he not loved the labor of painting the ceiling of the Sistine Chapel while lying on his back on makeshift scaffolding, would he have completed this four-year solitary project? Despite his complaints, the artist experienced a profound joy in the work of creation.

Michelangelo chided his fellow Christian artists for their failure to communicate the great joy of the risen Christ. They were far too preoccupied, he said, with presenting the horrors of the crucifixion as though the cross were the last word. They should instead be celebrating the victory of Christ over death and evil in all its guises.

In his "Remarks to Fellow Christian Painters" (1564), the greatest artist the world has ever known commented:

49

That is the tonic we need to keep us healthy, the
trumpet blast to fire our blood and send us
crowding in behind our Master, swinging happily
upon our way, laughing and singing and recklessly
unafraid because the feel of victory is in the air, and
our hearts thrill to it![2]

## Defining Our Thematic Context

On Day Two Hildegard of Bingen urged us to become
feathers on the breath of God. When we trust humbly in
our Creator, finding God wherever we sense the divine
presence in the natural world, we are loosening the grip
of those negative forces that weigh us down. Hildegard,
by her example, awakened us to physical beauty as an
incentive to love, hope and trust. She reminded us that
our stewardship of the earth should begin with caring for
our bodies in ways that keep us as healthy and
wholesome as our circumstances allow.

Today Mother Hildegard and Father Hopkins will
share insights into the creative process as a healing
ministry to oneself and others. They will spur us to create
(poems, gardens, pottery, songs, paintings, clothing,
prints, stews, pendants, dances, paragraphs and
performances). They will call us to relish this juice and
joy.

## Opening Prayer

Sainted singers, poet-pair,
Sing us out of boredom's snare

Beyond greyness, grief and tomb
Out where Easter-rapture's strewn

Stir embers of latent craft
Arise our souls to dance and laugh

Shelter flame of artist's bent
Call forth skills Creator lent.

Creator God! Make us gainful
Wet, joyful, green and playful!

Amen, Master-Maker.
Amen, Gerard and Hildegard.

Let the retreat continue.


# RETREAT SESSION THREE

Today our mentors enter together, side by side, both
in black; she the ruddier, he the more elusive. Their
contrasting appearances engender speculation: Will they
complement or contradict each other? What insights will
the play of their brilliant minds and ardent spirits spin off
for us? We anticipate the dialogue between Hildegard
and Hopkins. Their combined holiness gives off the scent
of dew-laden Rhineland grasses and the "dearest
freshness" of the earth in North Wales.

As it takes one prizefighter to appreciate the pain and
primitive glory known by another, so it is with artists
whose work is rooted in Christ. Hopkins and Hildegard
sense each other's toils, doubts, convictions of
unworthiness; they know each other's joy in giving birth
to a poem, a song, a sermon, a painting, a play. They
relish the joy of Isaiah's prophecy:

Thus says the LORD...

I am about to do a new thing;
   now it springs forth, do you not perceive it?
   (43:16, 19)

Eager to perceive it, we listen as our mentors begin.

Hildegard invites Hopkins to be seated next to her. He perches on his chair, eying her with the acuity of the kestrel. "Daughters and sons," she says, "listen: The tree of my life did not bear fruit until I gave up my poor feminine feelings of inadequacy and my fears about the evil opinions of others. When the living Light commanded that I write what I saw and heard in my visions, I took to my bed with one ailment after another. My health fell prey to my irresolve. False humility restrained me from communicating the wondrous visions I saw with my innermost eyes. There was nothing pallid or dreamlike about these visions. They were more like a burning light that invaded my mind. As I have previously described it:

> Like a flame which does not burn but rather
> enkindles, it inflamed my heart and my breast, just
> as the sun warms something with its rays. And I was
> able to understand books suddenly, the psaltery
> clearly, the evangelists and the volumes of the Old
> and New Testaments...."[3]

Hildegard explains that had she not been driven by grace and abetted by Volmar and Richardis, she might have remained "pressed down by the scourge of God." She has no doubt that physical illness of the type she experienced can be caused by spiritual blockages. For as soon as she agreed to release her visions, she "became healthy with a received strength." Even so, it took ten years of concentrated labor to bring *Know the Ways* to completion.

God gives the power of creativity. Yet the artist must be the willing cocreator. Had Hildegard not spent long hours dictating her visions to Volmar and describing them in graphic detail to the nun-illustrators, *Know the Ways* would have been stillborn.

Lest we minimize the extent of Hildegard's infirmities (thereby giving God less glory than is due), she recalls that she lived "with painful illnesses as if caught in a net"; the pain penetrated her entire body. To collapse from exhaustion or nervous prostration was not unusual for her. She was very susceptible to the weather, describing herself as an "airy person." Yet when she was rapt by nature or worship or creative performance, she was suffused with joy.

The living Light had revealed to Hildegard that God honored all of humanity with the "vocation of creation." Thus, whatever the cost of the creative process in our lives, we are not free to suppress the artist within. Our mentor comments:

> When a forest does not green vigorously,
> then it is no longer a forest.
> When a tree does not blossom,
> it can not bear fruit.
> Likewise a person can not be fruitful
> without the greening power of faith,
> and an understanding of scripture.[4]

If we desire a green and juicy spirituality, the well must always be replenished by the living waters of Scripture. Whether we work with words or seeds, wood or fabrics, paints or chords, our spirits need to drink at the "bubbling fountain."

Hopkins earnestly agrees. He recalls how his study of the Gospels and his liturgical prayer had intensified his love for Christ. "The more I knew of him, the more I wanted to know," our mentor observes. "Although in the beginning I had resolved to give up all beauty and the making of poems for Christ's sake, he later made it clear through my religious superior that I was to freely express the faith that had become my life. I was to allow 'all this juice and all this joy'[5] to flow out as praise and gift."

Noting the uncharacteristic color in Hopkins' face, Hildegard interjects, "Go on, dear Gerard. Speak to us in a Christ-poem. The singularity of your work is high praise to God and privilege to us. School us in the cadences that your Hero has inspired in you." (She remembers that he once admitted how sweet it was to be "a little flattered," as long as one does not cling to the approval of others.)

Our Jesuit director explains that the poem he is about to "perform" (his word) expresses his love for Christ as well as his allegiance to the medieval Franciscan philosopher-theologian, John Duns Scotus. Hopkins is completely attuned to Duns Scotus' incarnational vision of Christ as the crown of creation. For those who have eyes to see, Christ is reflected in every aspect of creation. Hopkins was likewise taken with Duns Scotus' grasp of the particular uniqueness or "thisness" of each created being. As Hopkins saw it, when the beholder of a bluebell perceives its special pattern or interior design, he or she "inscapes" the bluebell. To perceive inscape is to honor Christ as he is manifested in nature.

The poet bows his head momentarily, gathering his forces. We recognize this as a time of prayer. He speaks:

> As kingfishers catch fire, dragonflies dráw fláme;
> As tumbled over rim in roundy wells
> Stones ring; like each tucked string tells, each hung
>  bell's

Bow swing finds tongue to fling out broad its name;
Each mortal thing does one thing and the same:
Deals out that being indoors each one dwells;
Selves—goes itself; *myself* it speaks and spells,
Crying *Whát I dó is me: for that I came.*

I say móre: the just man justices;
Kéeps gráce: thát keeps all his goings graces;
Acts in God's eye what in God's eye he is—
Christ—for Christ plays in ten thousand places,
Lovely in limbs, and lovely in eyes not his
To the Father through the features of men's faces.[6]

Hildegard, warmed at the hearth of Hopkins' devotion, is
flushed and happy. The poet himself looks spent. He
seems not to recognize that more must be said. Patting his
hand, the abbess says, "With your permission, my friend,
I will venture a few words that may illuminate your work
for our retreatants." Hopkins is relieved.

"Had we not known you to be a good priest,"
Hildegard points out, "this prayer would have supplied
more than enough evidence. How painful it must have
been for you to be so misunderstood and neglected in
your lifetime. To craft a poem like this one, as brilliant as
a sapphire, and not to see it published or praised must
have cut you. Yet, as you yourself said, Christ values
what we create more than we do. He makes of it what he
will when he will. Once again today he is drawing souls
to himself through your words."

She turns to us. "Each singular creation—the
kingfisher flashing in the sun, the dragonfly skimming
the water, the stones ringing off the sides of a well—has
its own way of praising Christ by being itself. Each thing
gives out its inner quality of 'thisness.' In its unique way,
it echoes the response of our Lord to Pilate: 'For this I was
born, and for this I came into the world, to testify to the

truth.' " (See John 18:37.)

Hildegard adds that each of us, when we live in concert with our true nature, exemplifies Christ; that is our noblest calling and surest happiness. We are then in a state of grace; therefore, we do justice; we live in Christ and Christ lives in us. Our entire being cries out: "What I do is me: for that I came."

Nodding, Hopkins adds that even in the dark days when we are harassed by melancholy or illness, drudgery or loss, we can be "sad and happy" at the same time. He points to the example of Jesus himself. In pursuing his mission, Christ found his "plans were baffled, hopes dashed, and his work was done by being broken off undone."[7] Yet he knew the immense joy of doing what he was born to do.

Together our mentors rise, signalling the time for mulling over what we have heard. Each gives us a parting word:

> Every "poet is like a species in nature...and can never recur."[8] Whatever your gift, express it as praise to Christ. (Hopkins)

> Let the "juice of creation" flow freely through you. Know the joy of the Creator's kiss. (Hildegard)

## For Reflection

- In what ways has your faith brightened your life with the "feel of victory" or "the trumpet blast" of resurrection joy? Which comes more naturally to you: melancholy or joy? How have both experiences enabled you to grow in your relationship with God?

- In what creative ways have you expressed your personal

*experiences of God, visions of the reign of God, intuitions about holiness? Have Hildegard and/or Hopkins encouraged you to communicate your own particular gift in some new way? How might you do that?*

- *In what ways, if any, do you connect physical illness and spiritual blockages or crises? How might allowing your creative juices to flow more freely affect your health (spiritual, mental, physical)? How might you help others to experience the juice and joy of fulfilling their vocation as cocreators?*

- *Do you sometimes suspect yourself (or others you know well) of "borrowing trouble" or needing to be a victim of one kind or another? What needs in yourself or others might these negative mindsets satisfy? What advice might Hildegard or Hopkins give in this regard? Had you been a contemporary of Hildegard or Hopkins, what advice might you have given her or him on this score?*

## *Closing Prayer*

(To be experienced in a place where the work or the fruits of creativity have been experienced: a study, a garage, a workshop, an office, a garden, an art museum, a kitchen, a music room, a church. If you choose, create symbols of the juice and joy of your life in Christ.)

Choose one or more of these paired words of wisdom—from the word of God and the works of Hildegard of Bingen and Gerard Manley Hopkins. Read, reread, pray and make the words your own. Ask Jesus to fill your well with his resurrection joy.

**From the Word of God:**
> Let the favor of the Lord our God be upon us,
> and prosper for us the work of our hands—
> O prosper the work of our hands! (Psalm 90:17)

**From the work of Hopkins:**
> He meant the world to give him praise, reverence, and service; *to give him glory*. It is like a garden, a field he sows: what should it bear him? Praise, reverence, and service; it should yield him glory.[9]

**From the word of God:**
> "Master, you handed over to me five talents; see, I have made five more talents." His master said to him, "Well done, good and trustworthy slave; you have been trustworthy in a few things, I will put you in charge of many things; enter into the joy of your master." (Matthew 25:20b-21)

**From the work of Hildegard:**
> For all the arts serving human desires and needs are derived from the breath that God sent into the human body. And that is why it is fitting that God be praised in all.[10]

**From the word of God:**
> ...[I]t is no longer I who live, but it is Christ who lives in me. And the life I now live in the flesh I live by faith in the Son of God, who loved me and gave himself for me. (Galatians 2:20)

**From the work of Hopkins:**
> It is as if a man said: That is Christ playing at me and me playing at Christ, only that it is no play but truth; that is Christ *being me* and me being Christ.[11]

## Notes

1 Daniel J. Boorstin, *The Creators: A History of Heroes of the Imagination* (New York: Random House, 1992), p. 418.

2 Michelangelo quoted in *Joyful Noiseletter* (Portage, Mich.: Fellowship of Merry Christians), June-July 1994, p. 4.

3 *Hildegard of Bingen's Scivias*, trans. Bruce Hozeski (Sante Fe, N.M.: Bear & Co., 1986), p. 2.

4 Uhlein, p. 62.

5 "Spring," *Poems*, p. 71.

6 Untitled, ibid., p. 95.

7 *Letters*, pp. 232-233.

8 John Robinson, *In Extremity: A Study of Gerard Manley Hopkins* (Cambridge: Cambridge University Press, 1978), p. 59.

9 *Sermons*, p. 124.

10 *Book of Divine Works*, p. 359.

11 *Sermons*, p. 92.

# DAY FOUR
## Making Music to the Lord

### Coming Together in the Spirit

Louis was dying. For the last several years of his life, he had spent most of his time in a wheelchair. Stricken as an adult with muscular dystrophy, he had decided not to let the disease rule him. When asked to take on the directorship of a school of lay ministry training, Louis saw no reason why he should not accept it. Previously he had seen his considerable leadership skills as giving him a right to lead. Now he saw them as a source of obligation to do whatever he could to empower others to develop their gifts in the Church.

On his deathbed, Louis had the consolation of knowing that the lay ministry school would flourish even after he was gone. But a much greater consolation was the presence of his wife, Lorraine, and their five children. When their pastor, Father Louis B., arrived, he immediately anointed and absolved Louis, whose breathing was hardly perceptible. The priest proclaimed the Gospel his friend would have heard in church that weekend: "He calls his own sheep by name and leads them out...." (See John 10:3.)

Then silence enveloped the little community. Louis stopped breathing. Within moments, an unexpected sound raised the hair on the back of the pastor's neck.

Here I am, Lord.
Is it I, Lord?*

Lorraine was singing a hymn by Daniel Schutte, based on
Isaiah 6 (the prophet's call in the temple). The song had
been sung by the parish family throughout Lent and was
a favorite of Louis'. Everyone around the bedside joined
in; no one allowed sobs to stifle the song. They sang it
through to the very end.

Then Louis' oldest son, speaking urgently into his
father's ear, said, "Run, Dad, run! You are winning the
race! Run, run!"

Secure and transported by a song, Louis went on to
meet the Lord.[1]

## Defining Our Thematic Context

In our last session, Hildegard and Hopkins urged us
to relish the juice and joy of being creative persons. They
gave witness to the healing effects of ministering to
ourselves and others through creative endeavor rooted in
Christ. Today they invite us to focus on music as a prayer
so powerful that it can inspire holiness, rouse to deeds of
justice, defy the sting of death itself.

As Clarissa Pinkola Estés reminds us, our creative
abilities are an asset to be invested faithfully; they "give
outwardly" and "feed inwardly at every level: psychic,
spiritual, mental, emotive, and economic."[2] When we fail
to make the time and space for creative activity, we
become less human, less healthy. We are, in fact,

unmusical. Our song (or story) is our primary creative task. When we make sour choices, we sing off-key.

With Hildegard of Bingen as our director, however, we cannot remain long in that unharmonious state. Like others of her age, she believes in the spiritual and moral power of music; her songs feed and guide the soul. Centuries after her death, she is acclaimed as a liturgical composer of rare and unpredictable brilliance. Compact discs of her *Symphonia* (*Symphony of the Harmony of Celestial Revelations*) are sold through Catholic, secular and New Age media catalogues alike. Live performances of her opera *Ordo Virtutum* (*The Play of the Virtues*) are finding enthusiastic audiences around the world.

Those who have sung Hildegard's compositions often feel as though their spirits were being drawn out of their bodies. Those who have listened to her songs often experience a stirring, if at first disturbing, mode of meditation.

If we open ourselves to its potential, inspired music can be, as Hildegard would say, "a balm to every wound." And as Hopkins will demonstrate, the music of a sonnet can persuade us to have pity on our own sad hearts.

## *Opening Prayer*

Sainted-singers, poet-pair,
Conduct us in embodied prayer.

Expel your voices, worship, praise
Power the melodic, crafted phrase.

Wordsmiths, merge breath and thought
Chime out harmonies heaven taught.

Sound the trumpet of the Lamb
Ring out justice, help us stand!

Creator God! Breathe in us
Be our song harmonious!

Amen, Divine Singer.
Amen, Gerard and Hildegard.

Let the retreat continue.

# RETREAT SESSION FOUR

Gerard and Hildegard enter side by side; he carries his notebook, she an illuminated manuscript. Richardis von Stade is seated on a bench behind the lectern. Next to her lie a violin and an ancient lute, pear-shaped and pegged for tuning. We are alert to the promise today's session holds.

The abbess immediately puts us at our ease. "Dear friends," she says, "I sense that some of you are intimidated by the possibility that I might ask you to sing. You will protest that you know nothing about music—especially the kind I write!—and that 'you couldn't carry a tune in a bushel basket.' Fear not. Music is the natural expression of divinity in our humanity. We were all born to sing God's praises. He listens not for the excellence of our vocal performance, but for the sincerity of our prayer. As for me, your humble teacher, I have never been an expert in the art of music. As I have written about the songs attributed to me:

Untaught by anyone, I composed and chanted

plainsong in praise of God and the saints, although I had never studied either musical notation or any kind of singing."[3]

Hildegard is convinced that the making of music is a duty and a discipline, a prayer and a privilege for all Christians. She agrees with Clement of Alexandria, who wrote that the Lord made man a beautiful, breathing instrument of music, after his own image; for Jesus himself is the all-harmonious, melodious, holy instrument of God.

In her musical drama *The Play of the Virtues*, Hildegard presents a soul in contention between the devil and a choir of personified virtues. Performing or observing the play, she says, is an act of prayer in which hearts are softened, reconciliation is sought and the Holy Spirit is called forth. Any worthy spiritual music can rouse those whose ardor has waned.

> Even David made his prophecies good with music, and Jeremiah showed his lamentations with a lamentable voice. Therefore, o person,...listen to the sound in this music of fiery love coming forth in the words of this virginal youth who flowers like a green twig.[4]

Our director then advises us to learn to "play" the following instruments:

> ...[P]raise God with the lyre of profound devotion...
> [P]raise God with the timbrel of mortification and the dance of exultation...
> ...[P]raise God with the cymbals of jubilation...[5]

Hildegard urges us to deepen our desire for music by meditating on some of her favorite scriptural books

(Psalms, Song of Songs, Revelation), as well as those passages in which music is linked with prophecy, power and healing. She recommends: 2 Kings 3:13-20, Elisha Calls for a Minstrel; 1 Samuel 16:14-23, David Plays the Lyre; 1 Chronicles 16:7-36, David Leads the Singing; Ezekiel 33:30-33, The Prophet as Singer.

Although the abbess would not have been accompanied by an instrument while singing for the Rupertsberg liturgies, she has asked Richardis to play the lute softly here for our benefit. Hildegard stands a few moments in prayerful silence. She then sings in Latin *O Ignis Spiritus Paracliti* ("Sequence for the Holy Spirit"):

> *O ignis Spiritus Paracliti,*
> *vita vite omnis creature,*
> *sanctus es vivificando formas.*
>
> *Sanctus es ungendo*
> *periculose fractos,*
> *sanctus es tergendo*
> *fetida vulnera.*
>
> *O spiraculum sanctitatis,*
> *o ignis caritatis,*
> *o dulcis gustus in pectoribus*
> *et infusio cordium*
> *in bono odore virtutum....*
>
> Fiery Spirit,
> fount of courage,
> life within life
> of all that has being!
>
> Holy are you, transmuting the perfect
>   into the real.
> Holy are you, healing
>   the mortally stricken.

Holy are you, cleansing
the stench of wounds.

O sacred breath O blazing
love O savor in the breast and balm
flooding the heart with
the fragrance of good,....[6]

She encourages us to practice these few verses, invoking
the Holy Spirit to heal the wounds our sins have caused.
"You must sing," she insists. "God desires it of you."
(Those who do not have access to Hildegard's music are
urged to chant her words according to whatever simple
melody comes to mind. It is all prayer.)

Our director's face becomes stern as she recalls how
her music was silenced by the interdict imposed by the
diocesan officials of Mainz. They accused her of allowing
the burial of an excommunicated nobleman in the
Rupertsberg cemetery. She informed them that he had
been reconciled to the Church before his death. They
refused to believe her. When they robbed her community
of its right to sing God's praises, Hildegard was again
afflicted by a debilitating illness. With the prophetic
courage of a Jeremiah, she loosed a thunderbolt:

If on Earth they have committed the wrong of
robbing God of the honor of the praise which is
God's due, then they can have no fellowship with
the praise of the angels in heaven, unless they make
the situation right again through true penance and
humble reparation.[7]

By passionately defending God's and her community's
rights, Hildegard ensured her own health and led the
archbishop to recant the interdict. However, during the
months when she was deprived of her voice, the abbess

was burdened by a great sorrow.

Hildegard's co-mentor, who has been listening with finely-tuned empathy, places his hand on her arm. She in turn covers his hand momentarily with her own. "You know well how the soul is burdened when it cannot sing, dear Father Gerard," the abbess says. "Now give us a drink from your well."

Hopkins responds, "Mother Hildegard, I have barely restrained myself from punctuating everything you have said with 'Oh yes' or 'Ah but.' You have woven for us a fair nest of fleece, feather and straw; I fear my own contributions are nearer brambles and weeds wiry. Yet here they are: a raven's gift to a nightingale."

He expresses his envy of Hildegard's monastic life in which the chanting of the Divine Office (Liturgy of the Hours) seven times a day enabled her to breathe in the songs of angels and breathe out the hymns of humankind. Hopkins had always loved music. The life of a Jesuit professor, however, left him little time or energy for musical composition or perfecting his skills on the violin. He had laid on the altar, like a sacrificial lamb, his desire to feast on these aesthetic pursuits.

Hearing of Hildegard's rebuke to the archbishop, Hopkins had paled at the thought of such direct confrontation with Church authority. Even in the cause of liturgical music itself, he could not have done likewise. His high standards for himself allowed no hint of religious disobedience. Had his superiors told him to stop writing poetry, he would have bowed his head to what he considered an expression of God's will. Thankfully, they encouraged him to write. And he did so to "serve the cause" of his religion.

Hildegard looks pained at the constrictions this good priest endured; yet she is wise enough to know that God wastes nothing in molding his saints. Even Hopkins' self-imposed shackles could become the raw materials from which his "desolation sonnets" would be crafted. Although her thought might be "Imagine what a great saint-artist Hopkins might have been had he not lived such a narrow life!," Hildegard instead marvels at how such a brilliant saint-artist could emerge through a camel's eye. She reminds him now that his sonnets are his musical compositions.

"Yes indeed," he replies. "I did compose melodies for several of my poems. And I attempted to notate a few so that they might be sung. My invention of 'sprung rhythm'—in which beats rather than syllables are counted—came directly from my study of Welsh chime music. I dearly loved the percussive rhythm of one sharp Anglo-Saxon sound chiming against another as in 'new-skeined score' and 'pitched past pitch of grief.' My ears embraced such manly sounds and offered them as sturdy prayer." (Noting perturbed expressions on a few faces, Hopkins laughs at himself and quips, "Or so I thought then. As a Jesuit today, I would be far more sensitive about the uses to which I put my middle name.")

Hildegard calls her codirector back to the task at hand by inquiring about how the music of his sonnets served as balm for the wounds of dejection, chronic exhaustion and sharp-edged loneliness. Hopkins admits that he frequently suffered these strength-sapping afflictions. But worse, he says, were the terrible doubts about his own worthiness and God's mystifying sense of justice. There were times when Hopkins, like Job, loathed his life and gave eloquent voice to the bitterness of his soul (see Job 10:1.).

At Hildegard's urging, Hopkins agrees to share with us a medley of couplets from his sonnets of sorrow. Richardis accompanies him with a plaintive air on the violin.

My own heart let me more have pity on; let
Me live to my sad self hereafter kind,
Charitable; not live this tormented mind
With this tormented mind tormenting yet.

I cast for comfort I can no more get
By groping round my comfortless, than blind
Eyes in their dark can day or thirst can find
Thirst's all-in-all in all a world of wet.[8]

(Hopkins' ascetic face lights up the dark sonnet. He
pauses as we allow his words to enter our own dark
places.)

Not, I'll not, carrion comfort, Despair, not feast on
    thee;
Not untwist—slack they may be—these last
    strands of man
In me ór most weary, cry *I can no more.* I can;
Can something, hope, wish day come,
    not choose not to be.[9]

(Once again the poet pauses, looks directly into the eyes
of those retreatants he senses have been tempted to feast
on despair.)

Thou art indeed just, Lord, if I contend
With thee; but, sir, so what I plead is just.
Why do sinners' ways prosper? and why must
Disappointment all I endeavor end?
    Wert thou my enemy, O thou my friend,
How wouldst thou worse, I wonder, than thou dost
Defeat, thwart me?[10]

The pain in Hopkins' songs has readied our hearts for
reflection. He has given us a hard truth to turn over and
over like a stone in the hand. Making music to the Lord is

a vocation to be plied in our winter worlds as well as summer. Hopkins and Hildegard leave, arm in arm.

## For Reflection

- *In what ways do you make music to the Lord? How might today's session with Hildegard and Hopkins affirm and/or alter your response to music as prayer and worship?*

- *Consider the symbolic playing of instruments Hildegard recommends ("Praise God with the lyre of profound devotion...," page 65). Choose one or more of her "Praise" statements as a guide for your spiritual advancement. How will you play your chosen instrument?*

- *Which of the songs offered by our mentors today speaks most meaningfully to your mind and heart? How will you pray it? Invest your own creativity in it? Communicate it to others who will profit by hearing it?*

- *What might it mean for you to make music to the Lord in your own winter world? Whose help might you solicit? How might he or she serve as your accompanist?*

## Closing Prayer

(To be experienced in a peaceful place to the quiet instrumental music which is most appealing to the retreatant(s) as accompaniment for meditation. If you choose, create symbols of the ways in which you desire to make music to the Lord.)

Choose one or more of these paired words of wisdom—from the word of God and the works of Hildegard of Bingen and Gerard Manley Hopkins. Read, reread, pray and make the words your own. Ask the Holy Spirit to be the music in you.

**From the word of God:**
> And whenever the evil spirit from God came upon Saul, David took the lyre and played it with his hand, and Saul would be relieved and feel better, and the evil spirit would depart from him. (1 Samuel 16:23)

**From the work of Hildegard:**
> This sound [of songs of rejoicing] reverberates in all the works of good will like the full-toned notes of a trumpet. It carries in itself an all-embracing love, so that it is also able through humility to gather around itself the gentle and thorough compassion to be a balm to every wound.[11]

**From the word of God:**
> Sing to the LORD with thanksgiving;
>> make melody to our God on the lyre.
> He covers the heavens with clouds,
>> prepares rain for the earth,
>> makes grass grow on the hills. (Psalm 147:7-8)

**From the work of Hopkins:**
> Mine, O thou lord of life, send my roots rain.[12]

**From the word of God:**
> The LORD will save me,
>> and we will sing to stringed instruments.
> (Isaiah 38:20)

**From the work of Hildegard:**
> God should be praised with crashing cymbals, with cymbals of clear praise and with all the other

musical instruments that clever and industrious people have produced.[13]

## Notes

[1] True story used with permission of Father Louis Berube, retired priest of Diocese of Portland, Maine, and Mrs. Lorraine Bellavance, widow of Louis Bellavance, Auburn, Maine.

[2] Estés, p. 299.

[3] Gottfried of Disibodenberg and Theoderich of Echternach, *Vita Sanctae Hildegardis*, ed. J. P. Migne, *Patrologia Latina: S. Hildegardis abbatissae Opera omnia* 197: 104a (Paris, 1855).

[4] *Scivias*, p. 391.

[5] Ibid., pp. 393-94.

[6] *Symphonia*, p. 149.

[7] *Book of Divine Works*, p. 359.

[8] Untitled, *Poems*, p. 110.

[9] "Carrion Comfort," ibid., p. 106.

[10] Untitled, ibid., p. 113.

[11] *Book of Divine Works*, p. 313.

[12] Untitled, *Poems*, p. 113.

[13] *Book of Divine Works*, p. 359.

# DAY FIVE

## Being Each Other's 'Comfort Kind'

### Coming Together in the Spirit

It was one of those rare evenings. Everything went
right. The presenter of the Lenten evening of reflection
was cheered rather than deflated by the small turnout of
parishioners. Because there were only sixteen of us, we
could break out of the confining pews. We formed a
haphazard semicircle at the foot of the altar, disciples
gathering on a hillside to break bread. Each brought the
loaf of lived faith to fill the basket from which all ate.

Among us were two married couples in mid and late
life; one husband draped his arm lightly over his wife's
shoulder while the wife in the older couple rested her
hand on her husband's leg. There were two young Jesuit
Volunteer Corps members, male and female, agleam with
idealism. Likewise there were a liturgical musician, a
female pastoral associate, a male nurse and a street
person who spoke in theological jargon ("Like, man,
Teilhard de Chardin says we're all converging on the
Omega point. But who knows how transworld depravity
is impeding our ascent?"), and who walked off with
several unpaid-for religious books nestled inside his coat.
We were a diverse group, converging that evening into a

75

community of kindred spirits, sure that we had eaten at the same table.

Of what were our connections woven? Of laughter (poking each other in our collective Catholic ribs), of easily sung music (from the ecumenical Iona Community), of God's word (as it illuminates the reflection theme of "raising the dead"), of revelations (on God's dealing with us in our dailiness), of silence (in which seeds are watered) and of gracious coincidences.

These happy chances began with the director's last-minute decision to share a quote from Michelangelo. It was a plea that artists would passionately depict Christ's resurrection as a "trumpet blast to fire our blood." At that moment, the director glanced up over her head where two marble angels cavorted while playing their trumpets with obvious glee. As the others in the group connected with the angels, a young woman commented, "It's his birthday." The director, missing a beat, asked, "Whose?" Replied the woman, "Michelangelo's."

There were deeper coincidences in which one person's expressed sorrow drew out the hidden woe of another like a poultice applied to a chronic ache. When the director revealed her aversion to prayer after her mother's harrowing death, one man responded by speaking publicly for the first time of his father's recent death, also from cancer. "I didn't discover that I had a relationship with my father until he was dying," the man said. "Now I need to go back in memory and look for the clues that must have been there all along."

A second man approached the director privately. Her revelations about wrestling with clinical depression freed him to admit his own. Tears flowed as he confessed his guilt. As a soldier in the Gulf War, he had killed several people. "I can't forgive myself," he said repeatedly. "I just can't forgive myself." Yes, he knew that God had absolved him in sacramental reconciliation. But the ex-soldier could not accept the gift.

He wept silently. His depression and grief had driven his wife out of the house; she had taken the children with her. The director spoke a few words of consolation and prayer. She invited him to join in the local peace work of Pax Christi. She urged him to counseling, advised him gradually to let go of the identity habitual sorrow carves out for us.

Out of such exchanges, enkindled by laughter, watered with tears, the Three-in-One crafted our communion.

Our directors have challenged us to make music to the Lord in the summers of our content and the winters of our sorrow. They have shown us how music and poetry can become a prayer of healing, a path to transformation.

Today they will speak of our hunger for communion with God—a hunger that drives us to seek God's face in those around us. Hildegard of Bingen and Gerard Manley Hopkins suffered rejection, misunderstanding and loss in relationships that fed them. By the lantern of their witness, they guide us in the way of oneness. They will speak of how connecting with others can draw us into closer communion with God through Jesus in the power of the Holy Spirit.

## Opening Prayer

Wounded-preachers, tested-friends,
Witness to oneness without end,

Tear down walls we build between
Self and selves,

dry wood and green.

Rein in ego, harness will
Hold us fast in wholeness still.

Call to concord with our God
Cleanse deep hurts, urge to laud.

Trinity blessed! Thrive in us
Blessed communion of holiness!

Amen, Father, Son and Spirit.
Amen, Gerard and Hildegard.

Let the retreat continue.

## RETREAT SESSION FIVE

Our chairs and floppy pillows have been set apart, islands in the sun. Hildegard enters alone. She swoops down on her stool with businesslike intent. For the first time in our acquaintance, she practices monastic custody of the eyes. Hopkins enters from the opposite direction. He stations himself at a distance, as though constrained by Victorian propriety. His expression says, "There is no one at home." The warmth of our presession socializing quickly dissipates.

In her own time, the abbess gives us an inquiring look and says, "What do you think, my friends? Have we spoken to you as directly as the mother bear who rears up on her hind legs to confront an intruder?" Hildegard's love of drama impels her to impersonate the bear, erect and unapproachable. Our laughter pleases her, and we are struck once again by the child-nature which is never far from the saint's surface.

The abbess draws her stool up next to that of Hopkins. He nods in cool acknowledgment. "Pardon me, Father," she says, "May I join you?" In a stage whisper, he replies, "Oh, no, Mother, do pardon *me*. I was lost in prayer." To which Hildegard responds, "Ah, yes. I saw your 'Do not disturb' sign. But God-in-me refused to leave you alone." Hopkins smiles, takes her hand, and says, "Thank you for ignoring my sign."

Our mentors have called us to account for the walls we erect around our private and sometimes falsely pious selves. ("Something there is that doesn't love a wall," wrote Robert Frost. His fellow poets Hopkins and Hildegard applaud Frost's practice of poetry as spur to communion.) In this simple skit, we have caught the Sunday morning echoes of Catholics gathering for liturgy, attentive to God-in-tabernacle while ignoring God-in-neighboring-pew. Hildegard and Hopkins have tugged at our consciences, inquiring if we too may have preferred our devotions or our "space" to the possibility of fellowship when fellowship was not our choice. The abbess speaks:

> Human beings are vessels God has made and filled with the Spirit so that the divine work might come to perfection in them.... Those who long to bring God's words to completion must always remember that, because they are human, they are vessels of clay and so should continually focus on what they are and what they will be.[1]

What we are, she reminds us, is daughters and sons of God, companion sparks of divinity housed in clay vessels. What we will be, if we are swayed by the Spirit, is powerful and perfected beings rapturously enveloped in

God. To prepare ourselves for that blessed communion, we must see how we are all involved with one another. Even those who image themselves as islands must connect with the mainland for survival. (At this cue, we draw our chairs back into a semicircle, bridging any distance between us.)

Hopkins readily admits that by nature and profession he was inclined toward separateness. He belonged to a religious community; yet his singularity marked him off from many of his Jesuit brothers. At Oxford, although he had good friends, a few whom he longed to know better "despised him." His relationships were constrained by fear of rejection or criticism. He shrunk from the vulnerability to which his poems subjected him.

He shares with us an excerpt from a letter he wrote to Robert Bridges after his friend had criticized Hopkins' complex self-expression:

> You give me a long jobation [reproof] about eccentricities. Alas, I have heard so much about and suffered so much for and in fact been completely ruined for life by my alleged singularities that they are a sore subject.[2]

Hopkins further confesses that it was not only his poetry that was considered odd. His sermons were sometimes laughed at by congregations that could not grasp his meaning. His Jesuit headmaster at Stonyhurst transferred him to Dublin, remarking factitiously in his journal that he did not want to be held responsible when Father Hopkins went "stark-staring mad."[3]

Hildegard, too, because of her unique visions had been called "insane." Like Hopkins, she had feared the criticism of her contemporaries and been scorched by rejection. When Richardis von Stade decided to leave the monastery, Abbess Hildegard had accused her young friend of hankering after worldly honors. (Richardis had been named abbess of a wealthy monastic community.) She had tried to shame Richardis by speaking of betrayal and abandonment. She had clung to her friend, saying;

> Woe is me, your mother, woe is me, daughter—why have you abandoned me like an orphan? I loved the nobility of your conduct...and the whole of your life, so much that many said: What are you doing? Now let all who have a sorrow like my sorrow mourn with me—all who have ever, in the love of God, had such high love in heart and mind for a human being as I for you—for one snatched away from them in a single moment, as you were from me.[4]

But Richardis was sure that she was fulfilling God's will. And Hildegard had no choice but to let her go. Within a year, Richardis was dead. Hildegard wrapped herself in the cloak of God's mercy, remembering that God is the source and focus of our love for each other.

Through her friendship with the monk Volmar, Hildegard's faithful secretary, she had experienced the joy of a well-balanced male-female relationship. In the beginning, he was her teacher—the older, wiser, better educated Benedictine. But in her maturity, it was Volmar who looked to Hildegard for enlightenment. It was he who championed her cause before Abbot Kuno, he who accompanied her intrepid nuns as they set out to found a new monastery at the Rupertsberg.

Although she was a celibate, Hildegard had a deep understanding of the complementarity of women and men. Her nearly lifelong relationship with Volmar must have underscored the wisdom of the living Light in this regard. She shares with us now her view of the sexes:

Now it came to pass that man lacked a help-mate that was his equal.

God created this help-mate in the form of a woman—a mirror image of all that was latent in the male sex.

In this way, man and woman are so intimately related that one is the work of the other.

Man can not be called man without woman. Neither can woman be named woman without man.[5]

We are startled by how contemporary our twelfth-century mentor sounds. If only the warmth of her voice might be broadcast throughout the Church today! (A 1994 video called *Hildegard* depicts the abbess insisting that Volmar go with her to make the new foundation, despite Abbot Kuno's resistance to the venture. In Runcie's script, Hildegard tells Volmar, "I do not know if I can go without you." And the monk responds, "And I can hardly stay when you have gone."[6])

Drawing on her experience as a spiritual director to married women (as well as laymen and monastics) and steeped in the erotic imagery of the Song of Songs, Hildegard had written with holy passion of the ultimate connection between woman and man.

But the great love that was in Adam when Eve came forth from him, and the sweetness of the sleep with which he then slept, were turned in his transgression into a contrary mode of sweetness. And so, because a man still feels this great sweetness in himself, and is like a stag thirsting for the fountain, he races swiftly to the woman and she to him—she like a threshing-floor pounded by his many strokes and brought to heat when the grains are threshed inside her.[7]

As do many spiritual writers in our day, Hildegard celebrates the passion of bride and groom as a figure of our intended relationship with God. God is the passionate lover filled with desire for union with us. When we respond to God as does the stag to the fountain, nothing, not even death, can destroy the communion between us. Her face radiant, Hildegard proclaims:

> Set me as a seal upon your heart,
>    as a seal upon your arm;
> for love is strong as death,
>    passion fierce as the grave. (Song of Solomon 8:6)

In keeping with his upbringing and education in Victorian England, Hopkins observes that his deepest friendships were with men who shared his intellectual milieu. Although the poet-priest had a few good women friends (generally much older or younger), his circumstances did not provide an opportunity like that shared by Hildegard and Volmar. Hopkins was most dependent on Robert Bridges as intimate friend, fellow poet and trusted critic. Yet, because Bridges did not share Hopkins' conversion, their communion was incomplete.

Our mentor tells us how much he relied on the letters of Bridges, Alexander W.M. Baillie and a few others. Their letters were a "general stimulus to being" in times of depression and fatigue. They provided the kind of support Hopkins could not get from a beautiful landscape or even a well-made poem. As he once remarked to Bridges, "It appears I want not scenery but friends." (Hopkins urges us to resurrect the "lost art" of writing thoughtful, instructive and inspired letters to those friends who draw us closer to God.)

83

Hopkins' own greatest passion was Christ himself. His sermons spell out what his poetry so lushly suggests. Intimacy with Jesus empowered Hopkins; it kept him going when poor health, loneliness and frustration nearly killed him. Our mentor quotes from a sermon he wrote on communion with Jesus.

> If we do well [Jesus] smiles, he claps his hands over us; he is interested in our undertakings, he does not always grant them success, but he is more interested in them than we are.... We must then take an interest in Christ, because he first took an interest in us; *rejoice in him because he has first rejoiced in us.*[8]

For Hopkins, communion with Christ meant walking with the Lord whether to Nazareth or Jerusalem, Samaria or Calvary. The poet recalls how during an 1883 retreat he had meditated on Luke's account of the "walk to Emmaus" (24:13-35). Uncomforted and embittered at the time, Hopkins had nevertheless been able to rejoice in Christ's solacing of his disciples on the road and at the table. Hopkins saw that this comfort was intended for all of us who, at times, feel that we have lost Christ, lost hope, lost meaning. Rather than waiting for Jesus to come to him personally, the poet-priest had, by an act of will, taken the disciples' comfort as his own.

There were for him—as there will be for us—times when communion with Christ, either in himself or in others, seems unattainable. We must connect as we can; bear separation when we must. When we feel enisled or severed from the body, Hopkins urges us to reach out for the "kind love" we can "both give and get." He offers us the introductory lines of a poem.

To seem the stranger lies my lot, my life

Among strangers. Father and mother dear,
Brothers and sisters are in Christ not near
And he my peace my parting, sword and strife.[9]

The eyes of Hildegard, like the eyes of Hopkins, are wet. Although our saints now enjoy the fullness of Christ's company, they empathize with us in our need for the communion which is not yet. The two extend their hands in blessing over us, saying, "May you walk in the way of oneness."

## For Reflection

- *How have spiritual friendships made a difference in your life? In what ways have our directors encouraged you to nourish such friendships?*

- *What is your response to Hildegard's view of the complementarity of the sexes? In what ways might marriages and male-female spiritual friendships contribute to our communion with God? In what unique ways might same-sex friendships enlarge our capacity for communion? How have the Church's teachings on sexuality affected your spirituality?*

- *Have you experienced the loneliness, fear of rejection, and vulnerability we have seen in Hildegard and Hopkins? If so, how might they help you to transform such pain into power?*

- *Draw or describe your image of communion with God.*

## Closing Prayer

(To be experienced, if possible, with a close friend in whose company you feel united with Christ.)

Choose one or more of these paired words of wisdom—from the word of God and the works of Gerard Manley Hopkins and Hildegard of Bingen. Read, reread, pray and make the words your own. Ask the Three-in-One to hold you in communion.

**From the word of God:**
My heart is stricken and withered like grass;
    I am too wasted to eat my bread.
    I lie awake;
    I am like a lonely bird on the housetop.
(Psalm 102:4, 7)

**From the work of Hopkins:**
Each be other's comfort kind.[10]

**From the word of God:**
Make haste, my beloved,
    and be like a gazelle
or a young stag
    upon the mountains of spices!
(Song of Solomon 8:14)

**From the work of Hildegard:**
The fairest and most loving man appeared to me in a true vision, such that the look of him perfused all my womb with a balmlike perfume. Then I exulted with great and immeasurable joy.... At once, at the man's words, the sickness that had troubled me, like waters stirred to a flood by tempestuous winds, left me, and I recovered strength.[11]

**From the work of Hopkins:**

Break the box and shed the nard;
Stop not now to count the cost;
Hither bring pearl, opal, sard;
Reck not what the poor have lost;
Upon Christ throw all away:
Know ye, this is Easter Day.[12]

## Notes

[1] *Book of Divine Works*, pp. 338, 340.

[2] Bernard Bergonzi, *Gerard Manley Hopkins*, Masters of World Literature Series, general ed. Louis Kronenberger (New York: Macmillan, 1977), p. 103.

[3] Bernard Bergonzi, "A Dappled Soul," *The Tablet*, London, Aug. 13, 1994, p. 1021.

[4] *Women Writers of the Middle Ages*, trans. Peter Dronke (Cambridge: Cambridge University Press, 1984), pp. 156-57.

[5] Uhlein, p. 101.

[6] *Hildegard*, Omnibus/CTVC Co-Production. Script by James Runcie (BBC, 1994).

[7] Newman, p. 130.

[8] *Sermons*, p. 66

[9] Untitled, *Poems*, p. 109.

[10] "At the Wedding March," ibid., p. 52.

[11] *Vita Sanctae Hildegardis*, 3.53, PL 197, 127-128.

[12] "Easter," *Poems*, p. 45.

# Day Six
## Being At One With Ourselves

### Coming Together in the Spirit

His father determined that little George would grow up to be a lawyer, thus guaranteeing the son's financial security. George, however, had musical talents stunning in one his age. He was not allowed to have music lessons until a German aristocrat, hearing the boy play the organ in church, insisted that he be trained in performance and composition. Soon the genius of George Frideric Handel was no longer hidden under a bushel basket.

After the elder Handel's death, George Frideric tried to become the person his father had wanted him to be. He forced himself to go to law school. But he could not long suppress the gift burning within. He moved to England where he devoted himself entirely to making music, sacred and secular. In his adopted land, the young Lutheran composer's fortunes fluctuated with every change in the monarchy and the native competition. To an eighteenth-century composer, royal patronage was money in the bank. When Handel enraged leaders of the Church of England by writing biblical dramas for the secular theater, he was brought to the edge of bankruptcy.

George Frideric was a few steps away from debtor's prison when a friend offered him a libretto based on the life of Christ. The composer received it as a starving man lays hold of a loaf of wholesome bread. Commissioned to prepare this new work for a benefit performance, Handel worked like one obsessed. He ate little; he slept hardly at all. For three weeks, he never left his house. Once when a servant entered the room, he found Handel in tears. Like an enraptured visionary, the composer cried, "I did think I did see all Heaven before me, and the great God Himself."[1] Handel had labored mightily and brought forth *Messiah*.

At its debut in 1742, *Messiah* raised enough money to liberate over a hundred men from debtor's prison. When it was first performed in London, the work inspired England's king to stand at the opening notes of the "Hallelujah Chorus"—a custom of respect that has lasted over two and a half centuries. By the time Handel died on Holy Saturday, April 14, 1759, *Messiah* had raised thousands of pounds to feed the hungry, clothe the poor, care for the sick.

When a nobleman praised the composer for the "wonderful entertainment" the *Messiah* provided, Handel replied, "My Lord, I should be sorry if I only entertain them. I wish to make them better."[2]

## *Defining Our Thematic Context*

Hildegard and Hopkins each paid the price of being true to self; each has since been richly rewarded by the knowledge of how their works made the lives of others better. In their experience of communion, our mentors were strengthened to become the selves the divine Artist saw in them.

They have called us into communion with the Three-in-One as we experience God in spiritual friendships. Even those who, like Hopkins, seem by nature to occupy separate islands of creative awareness, need to connect with the incarnate God hidden in those who console and correct us. Our universal vocation is to be each other's "comfort kind."

Today Hildegard and Hopkins speak to us of communion with the true self described by Thomas Merton as our whole being participating in the life of God; it is totally other than the false self ruled by egocentric desires. The false self cannot be in communion with God. For how can illusion marry Truth? As Merton wrote:

> We are not very good at recognizing illusions, least of all the ones we cherish about ourselves—the ones we are born with and which feed the roots of sin. For most of the people in the world, there is no greater subjective reality than this false self of theirs, which cannot exist. A life devoted to the cult of this shadow is what is called a life of sin.[3]

Despite the labor and loneliness inherent in the task, Hopkins and Hildegard carefully tended the garden of the true self. From that garden came sermons, songs and poetry with which the wise might gird themselves against the unreality of sin.

## Opening Prayer

Moral teachers, learned guides,
Two homes where Three-in-One abides,

Expose illusion, translate whim
Disclose enshadowed life of sin.

Uphold lanterns to lustrous sham
Irradiate deft evil's plan.

Call to union with true self
Exhort to wisdom, inner wealth.

Trinity blessed! Thrive in us
Bright communion of holiness!

Amen, Father, Son and Spirit.
Amen, Gerard and Hildegard.

Let the retreat continue.

# RETREAT SESSION SIX

As his codirector sits smiling, Buddha-like, Gerard Manley Hopkins says he has an opening story to tell us. It goes something like this:

A monk named Fidelis was always striving to please God. He spent long hours interpreting the Scriptures, a work for which his inner eye well suited him. However, Fidelis was constantly harassed by the same temptation. When a fellow monk was praised for his compassion toward the poor or his eloquence in preaching, Fidelis began to doubt that his own service was pleasing to God. Jealousy of the other "more perfect" monks slithered into his heart. He even spoke disparagingly of those he secretly admired.

One day when Fidelis could no longer bear the cords of jealousy gripping his heart, he packed his few possessions and set out for a distant monastery. As he walked, a stranger joined him. Not wishing to appear inhospitable, Fidelis asked the stranger who he was, where he was going and why he was making the journey. His unknown companion replied, "My name is Fidelis. I am going to a distant monastery to get away from my self." Fidelis the First stopped in his tracks. His companion smiled and said, "Why long to be a pelican if you were born to be an eagle? And if an eagle removes himself to a foreign land, will he not remain an eagle?" The monk bowed his head, folded his hands in gratitude and returned home.

Having completed his story, Hopkins sits down in obvious contentment. He has always loved preaching, and is warmed by our attention.

"What think you of this Fidelis?" Hildegard inquires. "Is he someone you know well?" Without waiting for a response, she goes on to warn us of the dangers of becoming separated from our selves. When we allow sin or insecurity to obscure our vision of the person God created us to be, we open our windows to discontent and sadness.

Your spiritual attitude is like a slumber. I see in you a fitless inclination to slumber and forgetfulness. Wipe from the eyes of your hearts the restlessness of your spirits and shake off your sadness.[4]

When we forget our true identity, we no longer trust ourselves to know how to please God. Nor do we really trust God to prevent us from leaving home—or to call us back when we have awakened from our slumber.

Hildegard uses herself as an example of what a harvest God can reap when the sower is in communion with her true self. In our mentor's time, women were not called to the ministry of preaching. Yet during the last twenty-five years of her life, Abbess Hildegard was invited to preach throughout Germany. She undertook these troublesome journeys, each of which was preceded by a long period of illness, because she knew that the call came from the living Light. There was no use in her arguing with God that women do not do such things. And she knew in her heart that she could do it. To refuse would be to take cover under falsity; it would likewise be a failure to show her love for God's people.

In her sermons and letters, Hildegard exhorted believers to make amends for their sins against *Caritas* (God imaged as a beautiful woman personifying love) and *Ecclesia* (the Church imaged as a woman in white splattered by the mud of maltreatment by those who had sworn to serve her). She called prelates and people to turn away from injustice, immorality, worldly appetites and a half-hearted discipleship. She reminds us that we too must both heed and extend these warnings if we hope to live in communion with God, Church, self.

Lest she discourage us, Hildegard immediately adds that we have only to ask for the help we need in remaining anchored in the true self. As she says:

> In the world, it is possible for a person to do either good or bad.
>
> As a result of the latter, a body is placed in many afflictions. To lessen them, a person should therefore act according to the judgment of a spiritual director, lest one find only the bitterness and not the sweetness of life.[5]

When one of our number objects that good spiritual directors are not always available, Hildegard taps her foot and observes that the greatest Director, Comforter, Advocate and Guide is always available to those who pray. She asks us to join her now:

> O Holy Spirit... Bulwark of life, you are the hope of oneness for that which is separate.... Shelter those caught in evil, free those in bondage, for the divine power wills it. You are the mighty way in which everything that is in the heavens, on the earth, and under the earth, is penetrated with connectedness, is penetrated with connectedness.[6]

After a moment's silence, the abbess reaches out to Hopkins, takes his hand and invites him to continue the commentary. She is sensitive to his remembered failures as a preacher, and wants him to know that we affirm this aspect of his true self.

Hopkins' thin face is clouded as he considers that some of us may have to suffer, as he did, the trials of feeling unconnected—to God, to self, to others, to the fruits of our labors. The self he prays we will be in communion with is the one that has been transcended in Christ ("[It] is no longer I who live but it is Christ who lives in me" Galatians 2:20). It is this self that can patiently and humbly accept the dark night of separation. It is this self that knows suffering need not rob us of peace or even that happiness that lies in what Yeats called the "deep heart's core." Even though Hopkins' poem "Peace" implores the Spirit of Peace to stop evading him, he also says "I'll not play hypocrite" to his own heart. (In other words, he will not be untrue to himself by claiming that peace never settles on him; he asks only that when the Spirit does come, the poet can make the most of these infrequent visits to be strengthened for the daily trials of a life in which his true self is often blocked, frustrated or made impotent.)

To underscore the connections between patience and

peace in achieving union, Hopkins shares with us the sestet of his sonnet to patience. The opening eight lines of the poem address patience as a "hard thing," recognizing that this rare plant takes root only under trying conditions. The sestet continues:

> We hear our hearts grate on themselves: it kills
> To bruise them dearer. Yet the rebellious wills
> Of us we do bid God bend to him even so.
> And where is he who more and more distills
> Delicious kindness?—He is patient. Patience fills
> His crisp combs, and that comes those ways we
>     know.[7]

Hopkins' eyes hold us. Have we too felt this inner torment in which our sufferings and frustrations churn up rebellion against God? Have we too fought against our false selves, begging God to bend our wills to the good which is hidden from us? And have we too tasted the "delicious kindness" that drips from the honeycombs of God when we help to fill them with our own hard-harvested patience? Sensing recognition in our faces, the poet feels less alone.

Hildegard now stands beside Hopkins. His poem has ignited in her a desire to sing her "Symphony of Widows," women for whom our mentor feels a particular compassion. The often sudden and unchosen separateness of a wife bereft of her husband arouses Hildegard's desire to comfort these women who feel halved. (She sings only the second and third stanzas of the hymn which is addressed to "Father of all.")

> O first of fathers! Now we race after you with our final effort, delighting in penance (so lovely and so longed-for) as we sigh for your love: after our pain we devoutly embrace you.

Christ of glory, Christ of beauty! resurrection
into life! for you we left marriage, turned from
fertility: we embrace you in charity like the people
of heaven, O child of the virgin: when you wed us in
the spirit you divorced us from our flesh.[8]

Hildegard speaks to those widows (and widowers)
among us whose true selves could unite with only one
spouse. Once separated in body from that one, the widow
gives her embraces only to Christ, who has
compassionately divorced her from the desires of the
flesh. The communion of the two-as-one with the
Three-in-One becomes the union of the widow with the
Trinity. Hildegard implies that this union takes place
after the process of grieving has been fulfilled. Without
the fuel of pain and penance, the transformation from
halved to whole cannot take place.

Hopkins nods his agreement. He speaks to all of us,
whether celibate or married, lay or religious. If we would
live in communion with ourselves, he urges us to pray for
that "chastity of mind which seems to lie at the very heart
and to be the parent of all other good." He defines
chastity of mind, in this context, as discerning what is
best for us, "holding to that" and "not allowing anything
else whatever to be even heard pleading to the
contrary."[9]

Hildegard pats her codirector on the arm, gently
reminding him that his own rigorous fidelity to the
highest possible standard is not possible for all of us.
"Nor is it indeed wise for all of us," she adds, warning us
against that struggle for perfection that generates
unnecessary pain and heavy self-recriminations. She
seems to feel that her Jesuit friend was harder on himself
than God might have wanted him to be. Might he not
have been just as true to himself—perhaps truer—had he

given more rein to his good impulses for communion with nature, with friends, with fellow poets? She wonders if his depressions might have been less frequent and less severe had he worn his Jesuit identity a bit more lightly.

Hopkins looks slightly put out. Yet he has certainly entertained these same questions. He had committed himself to the highest possible standard, a standard which kept him always striving but ever convinced of his own inadequacy. Did Christ require perfection of Gerard? Or was it Gerard who did the requiring? Might communion between the priest and his Christ-self have been gained with less loss of contentment in life?

We are fascinated by these questions. Together with Hildegard, we encourage Hopkins to illuminate them by his witness. Ever honest in his self-revelations, he agrees to share some of his retreat notes made only a few months before his death in 1889. We recall that he was only forty-four at the time—a dedicated priest, a brilliant poet, a member of Christ's Company, some of whose confreres found him often "cheerful and unconstrained." He opens his notebook and reads excerpts from his autobiographical musings.

> ...[T]his is a mournful life to lead.... What is my wretched life?... [B]ut what is life without aim, without spur, without help?... I wish then for death: yet if I died now I should die imperfect, no master of myself, and that is the worst failure of all. O my God, look down on me.... [W]e want a light shed on our way and a happiness spread over our life.[10]

Like all who believe every hair on their head is counted, every tear stored in a flask, Gerard Manley Hopkins, sure that he had fallen short in fidelity to his Christ-self, wished for death. He fell under the weight of his "failure." He prayed for a comforting happiness that would not disappear at sundown.

Recalling her own depressions and sorrows, Hildegard understands well how Hopkins could have come to such a pass. Beyond the basic human sadness of being separated from Eden, there are many other travails for those who earnestly seek communion. When Hildegard had been laden with doubt about revealing her visions, she felt "only the unrest of doubt, desperation, sorrow and oppression in all things." The struggle sickened her, but she did not yield. She resolved to wage a "furious fight against it."[11]

Hildegard's efforts to be true to her Christ-self were not so much motivated by a desire for perfection as they were prompted by a need to know that she, "a poor little female," was indeed doing God's will. Whenever she herself or others thwarted the communications of the living Light, Hildegard became incapacitated. As she wrote in *Know the Ways*:

> If God's grace does not come swiftly to rescue the soul, this depression can develop into a spiritual paralysis and cause disdain, hardening and obstinacy in the human person. It fetters the soul's forces. When such a person encounters resistance, he or she is easily aroused to hatred and other deadly passions that murder the soul and leave it in ruins and decay.[12]

When we do not treat depression by wholesome means (a healthful diet, enjoyable physical exercise, companionship with creation, counseling, prayer and a commitment to healing), it can rob us of our longing for home (heaven), Hildegard says. The true self clings to the reality of God's mercy; she counts on the whale's spewing Jonah out on the dryland; she knows that Job's misery was not unregarded. The Christ-self trusts, and hangs on.

Hopkins and Hildegard invite us to linger over our reflections.

## For Reflection

- *What image or description in words or art would you offer of your true self?*

- *How do the struggles of Hildegard and Hopkins to remain in communion with their Christ-selves enlighten, encourage or challenge you?*

- *What means has the Spirit employed to keep you in touch with the person God sees in you? How have you cooperated with or failed to collaborate with the Spirit in this regard?*

- *In what ways have you felt "penetrated with connectedness" with God? self? creation? others?*

- *As you look back at this session's opening stories about Handel (nonfiction) and the monk Fidelis (fiction), what (if any) resolution do you wish to make? How might you see it through?*

## Closing Prayer

(To be experienced in a solitary place where the Spirit's movements can be detected by a wide-awake contemplative.)

Choose one or more of these paired words of wisdom—from the word of God and the works of

Hildegard of Bingen and Gerard Manley Hopkins. Read, reread, pray and make the words your own. Ask the Three-in-One to hold you in communion.

**From the word of God:**
> I bless the LORD who gives me counsel;
>> in the night also my heart instructs me. (Psalm 16:7)

**From the work of Hildegard:**
> For the living eye regards you and wishes to have you, and you shall live forever.[13]

**From the word of God:**
> Jacob was left alone; and a man wrestled with him until daybreak. (Genesis 32:24)

**From the work of Hopkins:**
> That night, that year
> Of now done darkness I wretch lay wrestling
>> with—(my God!) my God.[14]

**From the word of God:**
> But he said to me, "My grace is sufficient for you, for power is made perfect in weakness." So, I will boast all the more gladly of my weaknesses, so that the power of Christ may dwell in me. (2 Corinthians 12:9)

**From the work of Hildegard:**
> One is able to be saved through the bitter price of pain.[15]

**From the work of Hopkins:**
> I have no power, in fact, to stir a finger: it is God who makes the decision and not I.[16]

## Notes

[1] Patrick Kavanaugh, *The Spiritual Lives of Great Composers* (Nashville, Tenn.: Sparrow Press, 1992), p. 3.

[2] Ibid., p. 6.

[3] Thomas Merton, *New Seeds of Contemplation* (New York: New Directions, 1962), p. 34.

[4] Ulrich, p. 173.

[5] Uhlein, p. 72.

[6] Ibid., p. 41.

[7] Untitled, *Poems*, p. 110.

[8] *Symphonia*, p. 225.

[9] *Letters*, p. 182.

[10] Robinson, p. 143.

[11] Ulrich, p. 19.

[12] Ibid., p. 141.

[13] Newman, p. 31.

[14] "Carrion Comfort," *Poems*, p. 106.

[15] *Scivias*, p. xxi.

[16] *Letters*, p. 48.

# DAY SEVEN
## Seeking Rain for Our Roots

### *Coming Together in the Spirit*

Watching the Danish-made video *Babette's Feast* is like watching a painter produce a still life. The pace of the film gives the viewer pause: Have I slipped back into the eighteenth century? How long can I resist the fast-forward button? The film's content too seems anachronistic: no violence, no foul language, no illicit sex (or licit, for that matter), no dazzling special effects. Not an ounce of excitement in it—although a gourmand might well be excused for drooling as the camera lovingly ogles the feast. For those who do manage to switch to the slow lane, *Babette's Feast* becomes a meditation more savory than Coquilles St. Jacques with a bottle of Dom Perignon.

The story, written by Isak Dinesen, traces the gradual decline of a small religious community on the coast of Denmark. Two maiden sisters are pastoring the Church that was founded by their father. Its members have grown old and cold in their practice of the virtues. They occasionally cheat one another, gossip, complain and make do with a lukewarm faith. Like the dry bones in the Book of Ezekiel, they need a resurrection.

One stormy night a bedraggled Frenchwoman appears at the maiden sisters' door. She begs them for a job, but they cannot afford to pay her. Volunteering to cook the community's meals in exchange for room and board, the woman says, "If you won't let me serve you, I'll simply die." So for fourteen years Madame Babette Hersant prepares the community's habitual diet of boiled codfish and ale bread soup.

When the Church is about to celebrate its founder's one hundredth anniversary, Babette wins ten thousand francs in the lottery. She decides to spend all of it on a fine French dinner for the church members. Fearful of her lavish foreign menu, the community decides not to take notice of or talk about the food.

The meal is prepared and served with absolute artistry. Among the guests is a general who alone recognizes the uniqueness of the menu. He recalls a famous French chef who "had the ability to transform a dinner into a love affair that makes no distinctions between the bodily appetite and the spiritual appetite."[1]

Unaware that very chef is at work in their kitchen, the community members, bite by bite and sip by slurp, are brought back to life by Babette's heavenly feast. Their faces undergo a spring thaw; hearts overflow their banks. The diners' appetites for fellowship, forgiveness and love are appeased.

As Babette spends herself for them, the elderly Christians feel their roots, long starved by drought, absorbing her gentle rain. They are transformed.

## Defining Our Thematic Context

Over the course of our retreat Hildegard and Hopkins have invited us into a deeper awareness of how creation, creativity and communion can transform us. By sharing their sacred stories with us, they have reminded us that, as Isak Dinesen wrote, "All sorrows can be borne if you put them into a story or tell a story about them." Our mentors have shown us the beautiful child-face of holiness. They have dropped the shiny pennies of their wisdom-words to mark the path for us. By being themselves, they have proven the power of God in those who, though weak and inadequate, have broken through to communion. Today we enter into an active dialogue with our codirectors as they gather the strands of the retreat together, bundling the sheaves for the harvesters. They teach us how to pray for rain.

## Opening Prayer

Hawk-stalker, bright Hopkins, dear,
Feather-on-breath, Hildegard, seer,

Waken prayer, waft up psalm
Enjoin to nature's clement balm.

Gather tears in heaven's flask
Goad to joy; urge to love's hard task.

Hand in hand, join hearts and minds
Make us others' "comfort kind."

Jesus, Spirit, Father, One!
Rain on stunted roots undone!

Amen, living Light.
Amen, Gerard and Hildegard.

Let the retreat continue.

# RETREAT SESSION SEVEN

It is Hopkins' turn to present us with commemorative gifts. He is a boy carrying a basket of earth's bounty to share with his friends. That gleam in the poet's eye may seem dross to the distracted. But we are awake. We can assay the treasure placed in our open hands: a vacated thrush's egg, an apple blossom, a pear tree leaf, a golden finch's feather, a crown of mayflowers, a quaking aspen branch, a departed dragonfly, a smooth white stone, a single violet, green glass rounded by the sea, dried cornstalks braided, a ripe chestnut, a lark's nest left behind. For his codirector, Hopkins has strung a necklace of brightly-colored sea anemones.

She remembers hearing that the poet, aged twenty-six at the time, once gave his mother a duck's feather as a birthday present. Hildegard inquires, "Were you practicing poverty, charity or asceticism, dear Father Gerard?" Smiling his appreciation, he responds, "Oh, by all means, Mother Hildegard." For our sakes, he quotes from a letter he wrote to his mother on March 1, 1870, a letter that accompanied the duck's feather.

> But no one is ever so poor that he is not (without prejudice to the rest of the world) owner of the skies and stars and everything wild that is to be found on the earth, and out of this immense stock I make over to you my right to one particular.[2]

Hopkins finds it impossible to comprehend how we and our contemporaries can spend so much time shopping in malls for gifts when we could so much more easily apply our creativity to the selection, combination and presentation of creation's "immense stock."

Hildegard points out that our simple gifts can be chosen with the receiver's bodily or spiritual health in mind. Some of her suggestions may seem obscured by twelfth-century cobwebs. But each of us can find merit in the list.

- Find or acquire a sapphire. Give it to one who has trouble controlling his or her temper. Advise the recipient to hold the stone in his or her mouth to absorb wisdom.
- Give a sheepskin to a sick person or one who suffers from the cold. Otherwise, place large flat stones in the fireplace. Wrap them in towels and place at the foot of a sick person's bed.
- Help one who is anxious or depressed to plant a flower garden. Choose perennials so the recipient will always have new beauty to anticipate.
- Make bread of barley, wheat or rye for one who is undernourished or lonely.
- Sing and/or play a musical instrument for one who has lost hope or health.
- Anoint with aromatic oil the head, hands and chest of one who is facing death.
- Grow and dry herbs (tansy, mullein, feverfew) to be used in the bathwater of those who are under stress.
- Collect small stones of appealing color, shape, texture. Place in a leather or canvas pouch. Give to one who has bouts of nervousness (preacher, teacher, orator, actor). Advise the recipient to handle the stones while repeating a simple prayer, such as "Come, Spirit, calm me."

Hildegard reminds us that we do not need a medical

degree in order to practice the art of healing. She encourages us to study the word of God together with the environmental sciences. She insists that no one can exert the power of greening without being immersed in the Scriptures. When we falsely separate religion and science, we fail to use creation as God intended. Thus, we and the earth are afflicted.

Hopkins underscores Hildegard's wisdom by observing how often during his lifetime he was brought back to life by finding Christ in the inexhaustible resources of nature. What may have been a chronic low-grade depression sapped his strength and motivation. But time and again his health was renewed by experiencing the inscape of a flower, the beauty of the stars ("the fire-folk") illuminating the night sky, the tranquillity of fishing in a stream, the tonic of hiking through the countryside in Wales. For the poet, spring was always his restorative season. The season called him to contemplation and wholeness.

Hopkins recalls a particular day in May 1877 when he was able to enter into the childlike purity of Christ reflected in earth's innocent fertility. Hopkins had felt cleansed by the song of the thrush, invigorated by the sight of lambs frisking in a pasture. He had paused to meditate on the meaning of all this profligate beauty.

Together he and Hildegard proclaim the sestet poem "Spring," his voice riding above hers in a harmony that stills us.

> What is all this juice and all this joy?
>     A strain of the earth's sweet being in the
>         beginning
> In Eden garden.—Have, get, before it cloy,
>     Before it cloud, Christ, lord, and sour with
>         sinning,

Innocent mind and Mayday in girl and boy,
Most, O maid's child, thy choice and worthy the
winning.[3]

Hopkins reminds us that our innocence is withered by sin, as the spring flowers wither in the increasingly hot sun. Yet our contemplation of nature calls us back to the youthful purity of spirit so loved by Mary's Son. "Truly I tell you, whoever does not receive the kingdom of God as a little child will never enter it" (Mark 10:15).

Hildegard too is a child of spring. Her life in the lush Rhine Valley, her daily praying of the generative Psalms, her reflection on the revelations of the living Light have all opened her heart and mind to the *viriditas* (greening power) of Christ in creation. *Viriditas* recurs throughout her writing like a psalm response. To truly live and be healthy, a person must be green and vital, she says. Had it not been for original sin, humankind would never have withered. Human beings would have lived in a perpetual spring of "lush greening." Their spirits would have remained secure from the dry rot of sin.

By God's grace, spring always returns. And the sinner is invited to repent and return to the fecundity of a good life. Repentance and reconciliation are the rain that restores our roots. We are "trees planted by streams of water" (Psalm 1:3). Or as the living Light revealed to Hildegard, we are like a good field that receives God's word with a willing heart. Whenever we refuse to receive the seed, we dry out and our souls become parched. Hildegard quotes the living Light:

But the person dries up completely who has no intention of receiving my word eagerly and who does not want to stir up his or her heart to good things even though the person has been warned by the Holy Spirit and by the teachings of other people.[4]

The abbess is flushed with a sudden inspiration. Who has more to teach us about receiving the good seed than the Virgin Mother of God's own Son? Hildegard looks at Hopkins. In his perpetual attentiveness, he knows exactly what is wanted. They stand apart, facing each other, but drawing us into the space between them. With perfect timing and obvious reverence, they pray alternating lines from their respective tributes to Mary.

**Hopkins:** May is Mary's month, and I
Muse at that and wonder why...[5]

**Hildegard:** When it came time
for your boughs to blossom
(I salute you!)
your scent was like balsam
distilled in the sun....[6]

**Hopkins:** Ask of her, the mighty mother:
Her reply puts this other
    Question: What is Spring?—
    Growth in every thing—[7]

**Hildegard:** And your flower made all spices
fragrant
dry though they were:
they burst into verdure.[8]

**Hopkins:** This ecstasy all through mothering earth
Tells Mary her mirth till Christ's birth
    To remember and exultation
    In God who was her salvation.[9]

Infected by their spontaneity, we instinctively respond

with a concerted silence followed by applause and
"Amen's." Mary-love runs in us greening and contenting
as mother's milk. Hopkins and Hildegard are in their
glory—which is to say, in the reflected glory of the
dancing Three-in-One. We join them there in the circle of
warmth and light.

Our mentors invite us to give voice to our responses,
questions, insights or reflections on the experience we
have shared with them. Knowing our communion with
them and each other, even the shyest among us is eager to
participate in the dialogue. The Spirit moves among us,
lighting a candle here, scorching a lip there, setting a
spark to the kindling gathered since Session One. The
dialogue begins:

**Retreatant I:** I too love spring. But when I have been
betrayed by my spouse or my best friend, it's as though
my roots were being swamped by winter rains that pelt
me day after day. I lose the conviction that spring will
return. Prayer freezes up inside me. What can I do?

**Hildegard:** My dear child, betrayal is a merciless wind
that can dehydrate the sinner and the sinned against. Our
hearts grow brittle with resentment; forgiveness is
beyond us. Yet if we expose our wound to the Light and
allow our tears to flow unfettered by pride, God will not
withhold healing from us. We have only to trust, like the
widow before the judge, that justice will be done. And
justice is a gentle spring rain that will bring a new
greening.

**Retreatant II:** These inspiring thoughts fill me with hope
right now. But I seem to be addicted to worrying—about
my children, my grandchildren, our financial security,
our poor health. It's not that I don't have faith. It's just

that there are times when my worries suffocate faith.

**Hopkins:** Yes, I know the feeling well. There is a sense that we can do nothing to help ourselves or those whose lives are vined with ours. We pray for and expect consolation. Yet we cannot let things be and allow comfort root-room. We may write out our worries in a journal or a poem. We may air them out by taking to the sea, the woods or the pasture. But we must find a way to let comfort in. God is patient; so must we be.

**Retreatant III:** I have a friend who is hounded by chronic health problems. How can I help him to make room for God's comfort? Sometimes I think he is so identified with his illnesses that he cannot let go of them.

**Hildegard:** Be careful not to judge your friend, my dear. He may indeed be clinging to affliction as though to a familiar companion. He may, however, be a person whom God can reach only through suffering and weakness; thus, his illness is an aqueduct of grace. My experience makes me partial to those who have chronic headaches, back pain, depressive temperaments, insomnia. There were times when illness prodded me to the edge of madness. The "winepress of my nature" bore down on me. I had no choice but to throw myself completely on God's mercy. Encourage your friend to do likewise. Share with him the refreshing waters of this retreat. Pray that he will bathe in the living fountain of the Redeemer.

**Retreatant IV:** When my mother died of cancer last year, I was stunned by the toll of grief. Nothing seemed to matter anymore. I felt empty and uncaring. Do you think there is really any value in these trials that drain us of hope? Most of the time I couldn't even pray. How can that be a constructive thing?

**Hopkins:** Oh, how right you are to ask such questions! There were many times when I felt hardly human, times when madness seemed a refuge. But in time I came to see that when the darkness descends on us, so does God's mercy. In truth, God is most merciful when we are most tightly shrouded in misery. There is redemption in this kind of suffering when we do not utterly refuse it. We can be regenerated in the darkness that weighs down on us like the pelt of an animal. We can go on praying even when our prayers are like dead letters that never reach their intended destination. Grief can suffocate or spur to growth. Your presence here is proof enough you chose the latter.

**Retreatant V:** I have not yet had to grieve the death of a loved one. But I do grieve for the Church which seems to have turned its back on the new life the Spirit promised through Vatican II. If I didn't love the Church so much, I could let things slide and mind my own business, I suppose.

**Hildegard:** Oh, but it is your business, my dear. It is the just concern of every member of the Body of Christ. Do you think that I enjoyed having to correct and call offending prelates to account? Can you guess how many headaches those preaching tours and prophetic letters cost me? Yet what a coward I would have been had I refused to speak the truth about abuses in the Church! I felt it so unfeminine to publicly shame those shepherds who were so much in need of repentance. But I did it because I knew God willed it so. And because I loved the Church that had mothered me, I could not keep quiet as she slipped into corruption. Whether she listened or not, I called her back to the justice and compassion of God. So you must also do according to the Spirit's guidance.

**Retreatant VI:** The thing that rankles me is this gap between the real and the ideal. I want to be holy; yet I continue to sin. I want the Church to be holy; yet it is divided and divisive in so many ways. It's hard to hang on to the ideal.

**Hopkins:** Like you, I suffered the pains of thwarted perfectionism. I held myself to a high standard, and expected others to be better than they often were. I made Christ my hero, and was disillusioned when others failed to praise and imitate him. Even our disillusionment can become prayer if we turn it over to Christ and refuse to let it sour into despair. We must listen to the Comforter. It is he who rouses us and calls out "Come on, come on!" The Paraclete is our cheerleader. He signals us to do all that we can to make and to encourage spiritual growth. He pats us on the back and urges, "This way to do God's will, this way to save your soul, come on, come on!"[10]

**Hildegard:** Isn't that what the Spirit has been accomplishing in us these past few days? Has the Spirit not encouraged and instructed and goaded us on to the goal? Is there anyone here who has not felt healed by the balm of the anointing Spirit? If you say so, I shall not believe it!

We respond with laughter. Hildegard and Hopkins have endeared themselves to us. We do not want them to leave. They belong to us and we to them. The communion of saints is a closer reality than we knew. It is good to feel connected.

Our mentors call us by name to receive a personal blessing. The hands of Hildegard and Hopkins are laid on each head. They call on the Trinity to send our roots rain, to saturate our world with grace. Then to each of us they proclaim a particular call to be transformed through creation, creativity and communion.

In the end, they bless and embrace each other. Like Moses and Elijah on the mount of the Transfiguration, they have transcended time. They have come to converse with Christ in his earthly Body. And they have once again witnessed to the potential power hidden in the heart of darkness. "So also the Son of Man is about to suffer at their hands" (Matthew 17:12b).

So also must we who call ourselves his disciples.

## For Reflection

- *In what ways does the Spirit send your roots rain?*

- *How can you verify Hildegard's insights on the drying effects of sin?*

- *Did you identify with any of the retreatants in the dialogue? Which and why? What questions or reflections would you contribute to the dialogue? How do you think Hildegard and/or Hopkins might respond?*

- *What connections do you see between the opening story from* Babette's Feast *and the wisdom of our mentors?*

- *In what ways have Hildegard and Hopkins goaded you to joy?*

## Closing Prayer

(To be experienced in the place which the retreatant has found most conducive to prayer during the course of this retreat.)

Choose one or more of these paired words of wisdom—from the word of God and the works of Hildegard of Bingen and Gerard Manley Hopkins. Read, reread, pray and make the words your own. Ask the Spirit of Jesus to saturate you with grace.

**From the word of God:**
> All the trees of the field shall know
>     that I am the LORD....
> I dry up the green tree
>     and make the dry tree flourish.
> I the LORD have spoken;
>     I will accomplish it. (Ezekiel 17:24)

**From the work of Hopkins:**
> Trees by their yield
> Are known; but I—
> My sap is sealed,
> My root is dry.[11]

**From the work of Hildegard:**
> I [God] am the rain
> coming from the dew
> that causes the grasses to laugh
> with the joy of life.[12]

**From the word of God:**
> But the Lord said to [Ananias], "Go, for [Saul] is an instrument whom I have chosen to bring my name before Gentiles and kings and before the people of Israel; I myself will show him how much he must suffer for the sake of my name." (Acts 9:15-16)

**From the work of Hildegard:**

O frail human form from the dust of the earth, ashes from ashes: cry out and proclaim the beginning of undefiled salvation! Let those who see the inner meaning of Scripture, yet do not wish to proclaim or preach it, take instruction, for they are lukewarm and sluggish in observing the justice of God. Unlock for them the treasury of mysteries, which they, the timid ones, bury in a hidden field without fruit.[13]

**From the work of Hopkins:**

Above all Christ our Lord: his career was cut short and, whereas he would have wished to succeed by success—for it is insane to lay yourself out for failure, prudence is the fruit of the cardinal virtues, and he was the most prudent of men—nevertheless he was doomed to succeed by failure; his plans were baffled, his hopes dashed, and his work done by being broken off undone. However much he understood all this he found it an intolerable grief to submit to it. He left the example: it is very strengthening, but except in that sense it is not consoling.[14]

## Notes

[1] *Babette's Feast*, by Isak Dinesen. Film by Gabriel Axel, Orion Home Video, New York, 1987.

[2] *Letters*, p. 86.

[3] "Spring," *Poems*, p. 71.

[4] *Scivias*, p. 324.

[5] "The May Magnificat," *Poems*, p. 81.

[6] *Symphonia*, p. 127.

[7] "The May Magnificat," *Poems*, p. 81.

[8] *Symphonia*, p. 127.

[9] "The May Magnificat," *Poems*, p. 82.

[10] *Sermons*, p. 230.

[11] Robinson, p. 154.

[12] Uhlein, p. 31.

[13] *Sister of Wisdom*, p. 4.

[14] *Sermons*, p. 60.

# Going Forth to Live the Theme

A seeker after wisdom once climbed to the top of a mountain where an ancient seer lived alone with the Almighty. The wise one accepted the seeker with hospitality and invited him to stay for seven days. Surrounded by nature's majesty and refreshed by the stream of the seer's teaching, the seeker felt himself growing like a stalk of golden grain. His heart was large with good intentions as he made his descent on the seventh day.

Soon after returning to his family and his workaday world, the seeker stored his memories of the seer on the mountain in a file named "Retreats." Gradually he began to wither like a cornstalk in a drought.

Our roots have been watered by the wisdom of Hildegard of Bingen and Gerard Manley Hopkins. By their works, we have been instructed. By their witness, we have been healed. By their companionship, we have been heartened. What return shall we make to the Lord?

As each poet is a unique species, so is each disciple. No one but the Christ-self knows the pain each bears. Nor can anyone prescribe exactly how that pain may be transformed into power; yet God has made us in such a way that we can serve as Sherpa guides for one another. We need not imitate Gerard and Hildegard. But we do ourselves a disservice if we do not integrate their teaching on creation, creativity and communion.

The seventh-century seer, Saint Dorotheos, insisted in his *Directions on Spiritual Training* that there was no greater deprivation than to be without a guide on the way to God. He inquired:

> For what does it mean that where no guidance is, the people fall like leaves? A leaf is at first green, flourishing, beautiful, then it gradually withers, falls, and is finally trampled underfoot. So it is with the man who has no guide.[1]

The best return we can make to the Lord in gratitude for this time with friends Gerard and Hildegard is to do all that we can to remain "green, flourishing, beautiful."

### Notes

[1] Kenneth Leech, *Soul Friend: The Practice of Christian Spirituality* (San Francisco: Harper & Row, 1980), p. 44.

# Deepening Your Acquaintance

The following books, articles, videos and audio-resources are intended to help retreatants sustain their relationships with Hildegard of Bingen and Gerard Manley Hopkins. Additional resources are offered for those who want to explore the theme in other contexts.

## Deepening Your Acquaintance
## With Hildegard of Bingen

### Books

Fierro, Nancy. *Hildegard of Bingen and Her Vision of the Feminine*. Kansas City, Mo.: Sheed & Ward, 1994.

*Hildegard of Bingen's Book of Divine Works*, ed. Matthew Fox. Santa Fe, N.M.: Bear & Co., 1987.

*Hildegard of Bingen's Scivias*, trans. Bruce Hozeski. Santa Fe, N.M.: Bear & Co., 1986.

Newman, Barbara. *Sister of Wisdom: St. Hildegard's Theology of the Feminine*. Berkeley, Calif.: University of California Press, 1989.

St. Hildegard of Bingen: *Symphonia: A Critical Edition of the Symphonia armonie celestium revelationum*, ed. and trans. Barbara Newman. Ithaca, N.Y.: Cornell University Press, 1988.

Uhlein, Gabriele. *Meditations with Hildegard of Bingen*.

Santa Fe, N.M.: Bear & Co., 1983.

Ulrich, Ingelborg. *Hildegard of Bingen: Mystic, Healer, Companion of the Angels*, trans. Linda M. Maloney. Collegeville, Minn.: The Liturgical Press, 1993.

### Articles

Sanford, Peter. "A Saint for My God-Daughter." *The Tablet* (London) Vol. II No. 8016, March 26, 1994, p. 374.

Schmitt, Miriam, O.S.B. "St. Hildegard of Bingen: Leaven of God's Justice." *Cistercian Studies*, Vol. XXIV, 1989:1, pp. 69-88.

### Audio Resources

*A Feather on the Breath of God*. Sequences and hymns by Abbess Hildegard of Bingen. Gothic Voices. London: Hyperion (CD).

*Women of Spirit*. Cassette series produced by Jean Feraca for Wisconsin Public Radio. Tape #3, "A Poor Little Female."

### Videos

*Hildegard: A Woman of Vision*. Worcester, Pa.: Gateway Films, Vision Videos, 1994.


## *Deepening Your Acquaintance With Gerard Manley Hopkins*

### Books

Bergonzi, Bernard. *Gerard Manley Hopkins*. New York: MacMillan, 1977.

*Gerard Manley Hopkins: Selected Letters*, ed. Catherine

Phillips. New York: Oxford University Press, 1991.

MacKenzie, Norman H. *A Reader's Guide to Gerard Manley Hopkins*. Ithaca, N.Y.: Cornell University Press, 1981.

Milward, Peer, S.J. *A Commentary on the Sonnets of Gerard Manley Hopkins*. Chicago: Loyola University Press, 1969.

*Poems of Gerard Manley Hopkins*, ed. W.H. Gardner. London: Oxford University Press, 1948.

Robinson, John. *In Extremity: A study of Gerard Manley Hopkins*. London: Cambridge University Press, 1978.

*Sermons and Devotional Writings of Gerard Manley Hopkins*, ed. Christopher Devlin, S.J. London: Oxford University Press, 1959.

### Articles

Burgess, Anthony. "The Ecstasy of Gerard Manley Hopkins." *New York Times Book Review*, August 27, 1989, p. 15.

Egan, Desmond. "The Hopefulness of Hopkins." *The Tablet*, July 23, 1994, pp. 920-21.

## Exploring Our Retreat Theme

### Books

Dossey, Larry, M.D. *Healing Words: The Power of Prayer and the Practice of Medicine*. San Francisco: HarperSanFrancisco, 1993.

Green, Thomas. *A Vacation With the Lord*. Notre Dame, Ind.: Ave Maria Press, 1986.

Kreeft, Peter. *Making Sense Out of Suffering*. Ann Arbor, Mich.: Servant Books, 1986.

Wuellner, Flora Slosson. *Prayer, Fear and Our Powers.* Nashville, Tenn.: Upper Room Books, 1989.

## Audio Resources

*Creativity,* Thomas Moore. Kansas City, Mo.: Credence Cassettes, 1995.

*Poetry and Religious Experience,* Thomas Merton. Kansas City, Mo.: Credence Cassettes.

## Videos

*Brighter Days,* Series 1, Volume 1. Lofty Vision, Inc. 1993. Written by Muriel Foster.

*The Language of Life: A Festival of Poets* series by Bill Moyers, PBS, 1995.

*Spirit and Nature,* a film by Bill Moyers, Palisades Home Video.

*The Wonders of God's Creation,* Parts I, II and III. Worcester, Pa.: Vision Videos.